Research
Skills for
Teachers

ABOUT THE AUTHOR

Beverley Moriarty is a Senior Lecturer in the School of Teacher Education at Charles Sturt University, teaching Research Methods online and the creative arts internally. She taught in schools in Western Australia for a number of years and completed her Master of Education and PhD degrees at the University of Western Australia. She has a long-held interest in working with students and staff through their research journeys and into publication.

Research Skills for Teachers

From research question
to research design

BEVERLEY MORIARTY

 Open University Press

Open University Press
McGraw-Hill Education
8th Floor, 338 Euston Road
London
England
NW1 3BH

email: enquiries@openup.co.uk
world wide web: www.openup.co.uk

and 1325 Avenue of the Americas, 5th Floor New York, NY 10019, USA

First published 2018

A catalogue record of this book is available from the British Library

ISBN-13: 9780335249374
ISBN-10: 033524937X
eISBN: 9780335249381

Library of Congress Cataloging-in-Publication Data
CIP data applied for

Index by Puddingburn
Set in 12/17 pt Adobe Caslon Pro by Post Pre-press Group

BRIEF CONTENTS

DETAILED CONTENTS

FOR YOUR NOTEBOOK:
LIST OF EXERCISES

LIST OF TABLES

ACKNOWLEDGEMENTS

I would like to acknowledge a number of people without whom this book would not have been possible. I was inspired by co-researchers and co-authors Maria Bennet and Louise Wightman, who first shared their research ideas with me some years ago and allowed me to work with them. Their published works and their continued efforts now provide inspiration for others to follow. Professors Wendy Bowls and Joy Higgs showed me how to turn my long-term dream of writing this book into reality. Successive Heads of School offered their encouragement and support and a number of other colleagues over the years have also inspired me. I would also like to thank Sandra Rigby and Genevieve Buzo from Allen & Unwin for their encouragement, patience and professionalism. I am grateful to all of these people.

This book is dedicated to my dear brother, Raymond, who encouraged me in everything that I did.

INTRODUCTION

The purpose of this book is to guide readers through the process of planning, conducting and reporting a small-scale piece of research in education. The book is aimed mainly at novice researchers and students, who often have a short space of time in which to complete this work. If they have longer, then the process remains the same.

Educators are required to make many professional decisions each day. Many need to be made quickly and 'on the run'; others are not so immediately urgent. Some decisions relate to the act of teaching or to curriculum matters, while others are concerned with different areas of learning and development because educators are responsible for the whole child who is in their care for the full school day. Teachers' knowledge of their students and the school context, as well as school and departmental policies, figures prominently in many of the decisions they need to make. Just as it is not possible to predict with precision what will happen throughout the day and what decisions will need to be made, it is also not possible to anticipate with certainty the effects of such decisions until action is taken. It is the responsibility of educators in all contexts, including schools, further and higher education institutions and community education programs, to reflect on their actions and their effects in order to improve their practice. With increasing experience of a wide range of situations, educators are able to develop many skills that distinguish them as professionals.

It is also important for educators to draw on theories that have been developed or tested through formal research and the accumulation of research evidence when making decisions. To do this, they need to be able to read research reports and interpret their findings regarding what they mean for practice. Learning about how to plan and conduct small-scale research enables educators and student teachers to gain a deeper understanding of the complexities of teaching and to develop ways of thinking more systematically about the types of problems or challenges they encounter. The hypothetical example of the teacher who is concerned about getting students to write during creative writing lessons that is looked at from different angles in this book illustrates how problems are not always what they initially appear to be. To be able to think like a researcher is a valuable skill that teacher education degrees—both undergraduate and postgraduate—promote because it helps educators to learn to think more deeply about the nature of the problems they encounter and potential solutions to those problems. This book was written primarily to help teacher education students and practising educators to develop these skills and to lead them as gently as possible through the process of planning, conducting and reporting small-scale research about issues that matter to them.

Research is complex, however, and it takes much more than planning, conducting and reporting a single, small-scale study to understand the research process. Yet focusing on a small problem or challenge that is meaningful for the student teacher or for the practising teacher is a good way to begin this process. Learning about research methods is a notoriously difficult task, and teaching research methods is equally difficult; however, both can be very rewarding. For most of their undergraduate learning, teacher education students are provided with questions to address in their assignments. It takes quite a change of mindset for students to learn the process of developing their own research questions, yet this is a really important skill to develop. Poorly developed research questions make planning research, and even the ability to think systematically about problems or challenges, an impossible task. This is one reason why this book starts with two chapters that focus on developing skills for identifying problems and constructing good research questions around those problems. These skills are further developed and employed as readers learn about different designs and methods that could be appropriate to their research questions. The approach taken in this book is based on insights gained through many years of working with hundreds of beginning and novice researchers, and my passion for making the early years of learning about how to plan, conduct and report research an achievable goal.

The book guides readers through a process of identifying their own areas of professional interest—areas about which they are passionate, or ideas that challenge them or that make them curious. These areas then become the focus for learning. The activities that readers will complete in their notebooks throughout the chapters that follow will help them to learn how to think like researchers and to develop their ideas into research proposals and undertake and report small-scale research. Together with the highlighting of important concepts in italics, the margin definitions and associated glossary of key terms, the notebook activities signal the importance of taking time to pause and to reflect at strategically planned points in the process. This approach helps to deepen and consolidate learning, as it relates to readers' own interests and provides the opportunity to pause to think and reflect without interrupting the flow of the learning.

The book appears linear in structure, but it takes readers through a process in which they toggle back and forth between key ideas, just as researchers do. This iterative process continues until there is alignment between the research questions, the research design and methods of data collection and analysis, underpinned by ethical issues and dilemmas that need to be considered deeply at each stage of the planning, and the paradigm to which the research belongs. The exercises throughout the chapters illustrate the iterative process and encourage reflection at each stage in the research process. Readers are encouraged to re-examine their research questions as they work on their research design and methods, and to make adjustments to their research questions or look more deeply into the characteristics of different research designs in order to ensure that all areas are aligned.

The book clearly foregrounds the research question rather than the paradigm as an early starting point. It shows how, once readers gain some knowledge around the key areas in the earlier chapters, they are able to see how the research questions that they initially developed and refined, as well as their chosen research designs and methods, align with particular paradigmatic positions. It is argued that novice researchers are better placed to negotiate paradigms and the language around them once they have some background knowledge in the other areas—particularly when they focus on problems and topics that are meaningful to them.

Inevitably, every discipline uses distinctive language, or what students might refer to as 'jargon'. Specialised language connects people across the discipline and is important in the dissemination of research and its findings. We cannot ignore the reality of language, but this book tries to negotiate this area as gently as possible. The margin definitions and the glossary also help in this regard. Readers are encouraged to add their own items to the glossary as they undertake some of the further reading suggested at the end of each chapter.

Three research examples (two from student researchers) are introduced in the first chapter. Readers can access the reports of these published research projects. The three examples are woven into most of the chapters to explore how research is planned, conducted and reported and to consider other ways in which these studies could have been planned and conducted, thus enabling the examples to be used more deeply. Several other hypothetical examples are also used.

In summary, the book uses four distinguishing features to guide readers in their learning and to address difficulties that novice researchers face:

1. *Readers are asked to think about their own current or anticipated professional contexts,* from which they identify what puzzles them, what makes them curious, what challenges them and what they feel passionate enough about to pursue as a topic or problem to guide their introduction to educational research. These ideas then form the basis for learning about the iterative research process and how to think systematically about problems with which readers choose to engage.

2. *Readers are guided in how to turn their areas of interest into problem statements that form the basis of their ideas to move into developing research questions to guide later thinking around research designs and methods.* Readers are guided through processes to help them to articulate their problem or topic clearly and concisely.

3. *Readers' interests, which form the threads that connect the chapters as new concepts unfold are also built into the shape of each chapter,* in such a way that the areas of focus and the exercises in the chapters encourage readers to apply their new understanding to their particular interests and current or future professional contexts.

4. *Readers are encouraged to think ethically from the start, although a separate chapter is also devoted to thinking about ethical issues and preparing applications for ethical clearance.* The overlaps, as well as the distinctions, between these two areas are considered so readers understand that applications for ethical clearance to conduct research are not dealt with in isolation, but rather are a natural extension of ethical practice that is evident throughout all stages of the research process, including the planning.

Through using the book for their particular purposes, it is intended that readers will recognise how research is complex and how thinking like a researcher helps them to see practical situations in professional contexts in quite different ways from how they would previously have viewed them. In looking at areas of interest in depth as they progress through the book, what was previously thought of as simple may now be appreciated for its complexities, and what was previously a nagging, unsolvable problem can be seen as something that can possibly be approached in quite different ways than previously imagined.

OUTLINE OF THE BOOK

Chapters 1 and 2

Chapter 1 begins by talking about how to identify a topic or problem that is of interest to the novice researcher. The main focus of Chapters 1 and 2, however, is the research question. The idea is to learn about what makes a good research question and how to construct good research questions as a basis for then moving onto the later chapters.

Chapter 3

Chapter 3 is not the first time that readers hear about ethics but the chapter is set aside for specific consideration of ethical issues and dilemmas. Underpinning this chapter is the idea that gaining ethical clearance to conduct research is not the reason why research should be approached ethically. It draws the distinction between ethical issues and dilemmas, and examines what needs to be done in order to apply for ethical clearance to conduct research.

Chapter 4

Chapter 4 focuses on locating and reading reports of research that are available in readers' areas of interest. It also shows readers how to connect their research questions to what is already known and how to construct critical literature reviews.

Chapters 5 and 6

Chapters 5 and 6 are concerned with the broader framework and the type of research that the research question foreshadows on one hand and the finer detail about selecting participants and the type of evidence that will be collected on the other, in order to answer the research question. These chapters examine, respectively, different research designs and methods and what to do to ensure that the research question, research design and methods are in alignment.

Chapter 7

Chapter 7 closes the loop between the research question, the design and methods, and the research paradigm. Novice researchers often find it much easier to understand what is meant by paradigms if they have spent time first thinking about and planning the steps involved in the earlier chapters. When planning research at a later stage, they are then better able to appreciate their paradigmatic position at the time when they identify their problem and begin working on their research questions.

Chapter 8

Chapter 8 encourages readers to think ahead about how they will analyse their data. Further learning occurs during data analysis. Analysing data should not be like throwing receipts into a shoebox throughout the year and then taking the shoebox to the accountant to sort through at tax time. A much more hands-on and proactive approach to data analysis is needed.

Chapter 9

Chapter 9 gives readers the space to think about the implications of the findings of their research for practice and for future research. Just as readers will be influenced by earlier research in their areas, their research and what they find could possibly influence future research and practice.

Chapter 10

Finally, Chapter 10 provides helpful hints about predicting timelines, communicating with stakeholders, and conducting and reporting research. It focuses on how to write the different parts of a research report and what examiners look for when reading research reports. It also introduces a technique for checking and adjusting the content and sequencing of content in academic writing. This technique can also be helpful for writers who find that they are well above or well below their target word limits.

1

Getting started: From research problem to research question

This chapter will help you to:

 identify a research idea, topic and problem that you would like to use as the basis for your small-scale research project in education

 construct your first draft of a broad research question to guide your research and the learning that you undertake in later chapters.

Planning and conducting **educational research** is challenging, but it can also be truly fascinating and rewarding. It is easier to become absorbed in your research and to enjoy the challenges if you find your topic interesting, personally relevant and appealing.

Educational research
Involves a planned and systematic investigation or exploration of a problem or issue. The findings can help to inform practice and further research.

In this chapter, the process of identifying a research topic that interests you begins by asking you to think about your current, future or preferred professional work context and what you do, anticipate doing or would like to do in that context. Brainstorming topics or ideas that puzzle or excite you, or that you would like to investigate or explore, then becomes the basis for identifying one or more problems and developing related broad research questions.

Iterative process Revisiting research questions several times (iterations) to help researchers take broader research questions and gradually narrow the focus to develop specific research questions that delineate more precisely what the research will entail.

Small-scale research project This should be able to be planned, implemented and reported in writing by a single, busy, novice researcher in a short period of time—perhaps one semester or, for some students, two semesters.

In the next chapter, you will select one of the topics, problems and broad research questions that you drafted in this chapter and use them to develop one or more specific research questions. These specific research questions will then undergo a number of drafts, or an **iterative process**, and be further refined and become more focused as you plan your **small-scale research project** in subsequent chapters.

You will therefore have the opportunity to revisit your chosen idea, and particularly your research question or questions, many times—especially in the next chapter. It is important to think of your initial ideas and questions as being in draft form only at this stage: they do not need to be perfect.

In fact, this chapter is more about brainstorming ideas and less about polishing your work. This approach is highly desirable. It takes time to develop a compilation of ideas from which you choose your direction for your study. For this reason, it is important not to rush the initial stage of deciding on your research idea, topic or problem, or to try to narrow your problem and refine your research question too soon. It is also very important to discuss your ideas for the direction of your study early with your lecturer or research supervisor to ensure that your topic is suitable for a novice researcher.

This chapter also provides examples of previous and current research. These are not suggestions for topics that you might pursue in your research. Several topics may not be suitable for your research, either because of the level of risk appropriate for novice researchers or because your context is different. In fact, you should focus on research that carries a low level of risk until you have the appropriate experience. Instead, the examples provided here simply illustrate a few different circumstances that have led researchers to identify initial ideas for their research to demonstrate how ideas can be developed into topics, problems, broad research questions and purpose statements. This general process is applicable to all research planning, including research conducted in schools and research that examines the connections between policy and practice in schools.

To begin thinking about high-risk and low-risk research, visit the National Health and Medical Research Council Guidelines relating to research with Aboriginal and Torres Strait Islander Peoples (www.nhmrc.gov.au/guidelines-publications/e52). Such research is generally regarded as being high-risk and unsuitable for novice researchers.

You are encouraged to take the time to engage with the activities in this chapter, to think about what really interests you and to start a notebook of ideas and thoughts that you continue to build on while working through the remainder of the book. All good researchers keep notebooks to record their ideas, so you will be in good company.

For your notebook

Wherever you see this book icon and the words 'For your notebook', you will be given points to consider. It is then time to pause and write down your thoughts about these points.

Of course, thoughts can be more random than this, so it is good practice to keep your notebook to hand in order to record any additional thoughts whenever they occur to you and before they are lost. You can then return to them later without deviating from your current thoughts. For ease of cross-referencing later between your notes and the book, the 'For your notebook' icons are numbered according to the chapter and their sequence within the chapter.

GETTING STARTED: THINKING ABOUT YOUR CURRENT, FUTURE OR PREFERRED WORK CONTEXT

Here is your first opportunity to pause, to think and to write in your notebook. This task is important because it will help you to begin the process of identifying ideas for your small-scale research project that you find both relevant and interesting. You will return later to the ideas that you record here as you work out which ideas are appropriate for you and as you plan your small-scale research project.

 For your notebook

Exercise 1.1 Current, future or preferred work context

Write a paragraph to describe your current, future (anticipated) or preferred professional work *context* in the field of education.

Write a second paragraph that describes the work that you do, will do or would like to do in that context and why that work interests you, challenges you, puzzles you or just makes you curious. Brainstorm and note ideas that you might like to investigate or explore in that context. Brainstorming means that, rather than pondering too long over any idea, you try to list as many ideas as you can so that you do not get fixated on just one or a few ideas.

Label your response 'Exercise 1.1 Current, future or preferred work context' for ease of cross-referencing later.

HOW THE PROCESS IS RELEVANT TO YOU

In some disciplines, students are given a topic or a question to guide their research. In education, we often decide on our own particular direction, our own topic, problem or issue, and our own research question—albeit that in some situations, such as when you are studying a semester-long course or subject, you are given broad parameters within which your research needs to fit. Even then, you often still need to identify the small part of the puzzle that you wish to be your focus. You may be required to work individually or to undertake research in a small group. You should take into account any parameters required by your studies as you develop your ideas and discuss them with your lecturer or research supervisor.

For example, you may be in your final year of your teacher education degree—perhaps studying early childhood or physical education—and you are required to plan and implement a very small research project of interest to you within that broad area. This means that you may need to narrow the focus and develop your own research questions within the boundaries set by your lecturer. Other students may be undertaking a research methods subject in which they can choose their own area of interest.

In subjects or courses where you are not required to plan and conduct research, the lecturer usually sets the assignments and gives you predetermined questions or directions. It feels quite different when you are in the position of developing (and refining) your own research question. Some students feel really comfortable and excited about the prospect of doing a project that is of particular interest to them, while others find it a little strange or even daunting for a while. Both reactions are common, and I have worked with many students in both situations. This book is written to take you gently through the process of developing your ideas, knowing that there will be times when you have your doubts and other times when you feel more confident.

Briefly, your reason for engaging in the processes dealt with in this book could be one of the following:

Quantitative research
Concerned with data in the form of numbers, such as scores on tests of achievement or when participants in the research rate their responses to a number of questions on a scale.

Qualitative research
Invites participants to provide responses that involve written and/or spoken words in order to understand a phenomenon or problem from the perspectives of the people involved.

- You may be required to plan, implement and report on a **quantitative** or **qualitative research** project within a specified period.
- You may need to learn about the research process and do some planning, but not to conduct a study this semester (although for some students the study may be conducted in a later semester).
- You may be required to plan and conduct a small study in which you trial with a small number of **research**

participants an instrument such as a questionnaire or interview questions that you develop (an **interview schedule or interview guide**) and to report on your trial.

- Participants in quantitative research are sometimes called 'subjects', but many researchers prefer to call them 'participants'. Depending on their orientation, researchers may see subjects as the people on whom their research is conducted or participants as the people with and for whom their research is conducted.

- Other students may need to plan small, low-risk projects to implement while on their practical placements in schools, classrooms, school libraries or other educational contexts.

- Some students may be undertaking a minor thesis/capstone subject, an Honours year, a graduate certificate in educational research or research subjects or courses for a Master's degree.

Research participants
The people from whom evidence or data are gathered. Participants in quantitative research (in which data are in the form of numbers) are sometimes called subjects.

Interview schedule or interview guide A set of questions developed and used to conduct interviews with people who participate in the research. The questions are designed in such a way that the responses will inform or answer your research questions.

The process is the same in each case; the difference is how far through the book you need to work.

It is important for all novice researchers to consult closely with their lecturers or research supervisors from the beginning to ensure that their projects are low-risk, avoid the involvement of participants who could be considered to be vulnerable, and are mindful of potential power relationships between teacher and student. These points will be raised as you decide on the direction you will take in your research and work through your plans with your lecturer. Your research should potentially only involve participants who have the capacity to decide whether they wish to be involved. Participation in your research must be voluntary, as exceptions to this approach are rarely accepted in educational research.

 For your notebook

Exercise 1.2 Requirements of your subject or course

Take a moment to check the requirements of your subject or course and *note or highlight* the key points. This will help to keep you on track as you work through this book and keep your study relevant and focused. In particular, note any advice about ensuring that your research is likely to be in a lower risk category and will not involve participants who could be considered vulnerable.

Check the Table of Contents at the front of this book, the brief description of each chapter in the Introduction and the objectives at the start of each chapter to determine which chapters might be relevant to you. If you have not done so already, read the introduction to the book—this is an appropriate time to undertake this task.

If you are required to develop ideas for or plan a piece of research but not to conduct it, then some chapters will be more relevant to you than others. If you are required to plan, implement and report the findings of your research, then you will work your way through all the chapters with similar intensity.

Allowing yourself plenty of time to think and plan what you will do and to get your ideas focused and specific enough to make them manageable for a busy, novice researcher is important. You need time to discuss your ideas with your lecturer or supervisor, to take advice and to develop your confidence. Some students may normally prefer to proceed more quickly, while others will take more time. Learning about the research process is all about finding a comfortable and working balance between the two, *while also ensuring that the project is not commenced until formal approval is given.*

The best advice is to 'hit the road running'. Starting the process early and choosing a topic that you find interesting, relevant, useful or challenging, and about which you are curious and passionate, is just as important as consulting with your lecturer about the suitability of your topic.

THE ORIGINS OF RESEARCH IDEAS AND RESEARCH QUESTIONS

This section of the chapter provides background information about a few very different research projects and how they started. We will return to these projects at different places throughout the book as you progressively work through the processes involved in refining your research question and thinking about how you will design your study and the methods that you will use for **data** collection and analysis, right through to how you will report your study.

Data The evidence or information collected or generated in order to answer the research question/s.

Data could be the responses from the participants, such as what they say when interviewed or when completing a survey, or it could be the information generated when classrooms are observed. Data collection and data generation and the methods used to analyse the data are planned carefully ahead of time.

Research starts with an idea that can come from almost anywhere. Here are three examples. Note that you were asked to think of a few ideas of your own first and write them down in your notebook in Exercise 1.1. Looking at examples before doing such an exercise can sometimes constrain your thinking rather than encourage you to expand your horizons and think creatively.

Example 1: Student project—evaluation of a program

Louise Wightman, a student who worked at a community centre, designed an education program to support young parents or prospective parents in the early stages of parenthood. Louise delivered parts of the program and arranged for other professionals to deliver the remaining parts. She was keen to find out from the participants in the program what they thought about both the content of the program and how it was delivered so that strengths and ways to enhance the program could be identified. Her research therefore evaluated the content and delivery of the program from the perspectives of the participants (Wightman & Moriarty, 2012).

- Louise's broad *topic* was 'community education programs for young parents and young prospective parents'.
- The *problem* that interested Louise was a practical one related to making decisions about the content and delivery of education programs to meet the needs of young parents and prospective parents.
- A *broad research question* around the above scenario could be: 'What do young parents and prospective

young parents look for in community education programs designed to help them adjust to parenthood?'

- The *purpose* of Louise's research was therefore to identify from the perspectives of participants in an education program for young parents strengths and areas for further enhancement in the content and delivery of the program that she had designed.
- This was a *small–scale study* conducted by an education student who had never previously conducted research. In later chapters, we will draw more generally on this research direction to show how an interest in the education of a particular group can be the catalyst for a number of possible small-scale research projects of a size that is manageable for a single, novice researcher.

Before reading Example 2, you may wish to visit the link to the Australian Professional Standards for Teachers on the Australian Institute for Teaching and School Leadership website (www.aitsl.edu.au/teach/standards). Maria's research below relates to Standard 1.4: *Strategies for teaching Aboriginal and Torres Strait Islander Students* and Standard 2.4: *Understand and respect Aboriginal and Torres Strait Islander people to promote reconciliation between Indigenous and non-Indigenous Australians.* As you continue to develop your own ideas for a small-scale study, you may see links between your topic and the Professional Standards.

Example 2: Concerns of pre-service teachers

A group of pre-service teacher education students were worried about how to teach Aboriginal students on their forthcoming teaching practice and later as practising teachers. The pre-service teachers expressed their concerns to one of their university lecturers, Maria Bennet. In partnership with the local Aboriginal community, Maria provided a series of scaffolded experiences to help the pre-service teachers to connect with their local Aboriginal community and learn how to teach reading at an Aboriginal after-school community centre. A research project to evaluate the experiences began (Bennet & Lancaster, 2012).

- Maria's broad *topic* was 'preparing pre-service teachers to connect with and teach Aboriginal students'.
- Maria's problem was a practical one. It arose from the concerns of pre-service teachers about how they would teach Aboriginal students while on their practical placements and later as practising teachers.
- A simple, broad research question to guide a project such as this one could be: 'How can pre-service teachers gain the knowledge and skills to teach Aboriginal students?'
- The purpose of Maria's research was therefore to evaluate a program or intervention intended to help pre-service teachers begin to develop the knowledge and skills needed to teach Aboriginal students.

We will follow Maria's research as it develops and also consider throughout the book different ways in which it could have been designed as a small-scale study, equivalent in size to what you might be thinking about in your particular area of interest.

You may have similar concerns to the pre-service teachers in the example above, in that you may be wondering how you will be able to teach a particular group of students or a particular subject. For example, imagine that you would like to find out more about how to extend the learning of children who are gifted or to develop your skills in teaching fractions.

This research project later developed into a **longitudinal study** involving practising teachers in their fifth year of teaching and who were the participants in the initial phase of the study (Moriarty & Bennet, 2016). The research also moved sideways to other, complementary studies that developed out of the findings of the initial phase. In this way the different parts of the study collectively have the potential to make a more significant contribution to knowledge in the area. Longitudinal research is not regarded as small-scale; it is therefore unlikely that novice researchers will conduct longitudinal studies.

Longitudinal studies There are two types: the first involves collecting data from the same group of participants more than once over an extended period of time; the second involves collecting the same data from successive cohorts over an extended period of time—several years, for example.

The above two research projects involved interviewing adult participants or asking them to write about their ideas so that the researchers could explore participants' thoughts on particular topics using the direct words of the participants. The participants therefore articulated their ideas in words rather than in numbers. These are examples of *qualitative research*. This type of research is discussed in more detail later in the book, particularly in Chapters 4, 5 and 6.

The following example, which is drawn from my own research, provides a contrast. In keeping with our small-scale emphasis, the focus here is on just one aspect of a larger study. This research is quite different from the first two examples and carries with it a lower level of risk than Maria's research. This research is also quite different from Louise and Maria's research because no interviews were conducted and the research participants did not write their responses in sentences. This is an example of *quantitative research*—that is, research in which the data are in the form of numbers and measurements rather than words. This time, the participants were pre-service teachers who were learning how to teach problem solving in primary level mathematics. This type of research will also be looked at in more detail later, particularly in Chapters 4, 5 and 6.

Hypothesis Prediction about the findings of a study that is proposed at the start of the research. Generally influenced by previous research and theory, and usually relates to quantitative research, in which data are in the form of numbers.

Example 3: Confidence to solve mathematical problems and confidence to teach mathematical problem solving

A group of lecturers was worried about the confidence levels of pre-service teachers to teach mathematical problem solving to primary- or elementary-level students. A program intended to increase the pre-service teachers' own abilities to solve mathematical problems was developed. In the planning stages of the study, and based on self-efficacy theory, it was hypothesised (or anticipated) that when pre-service teachers were confident in their own abilities to solve mathematical problems, they would also be confident to teach mathematical problem solving to others. Confidence (or self-efficacy) in these areas was measured and the data were in the form of numbers. The data supported the **hypothesis** and a high, positive **correlation** was found between these two areas. (Note that Chapter 5 draws the distinction between correlation and causation and quantitative research designs that are appropriate for each.)

- The broad *topic* for this research was 'pre-service teachers' confidence to teach mathematics'.

- The *problem* was concerned with how to increase pre-service teachers' abilities and confidence (self-efficacy) levels in solving mathematical problems and in teaching others to solve mathematical problems.

- This research involved *measuring* pre-service teachers' mathematical problem-solving abilities and their confidence levels (or self-efficacy) for solving mathematical problems and teaching others to solve mathematical problems. Measurement implies *quantification*; therefore, the data were in the form of numbers and the research was quantitative.

- A *broad research question* that could be posed in this area is: 'What is the correlation between ability to solve mathematical problems and confidence to teach mathematical problem solving?'

- One *purpose* of my research (Moriarty, 2014) was therefore to calculate the correlation between pre-service teachers' confidence or self-efficacy to solve mathematical problems and their confidence to teach mathematical problem solving.

Correlation Refers to the *statistical relationship* between two or more concepts or variables. An example is whether confidence to solve mathematical problems and confidence to teach mathematical problem solving are related. This does not mean that being confident in one area *causes* a person to be confident in the other, just that levels of confidence in one area are *associated* with levels of confidence in the other area.

Research ideas therefore often start with curiosity—with a problem that needs solving or something that is challenging. Just think about some of the stories that have appeared in the media recently. It is amazing how often authorities or the public look to schools to help solve social problems, or at least to help children to cope with social or family problems that affect them. Examples include bullying and driver education. When schools are required to implement programs that target problems such as these, researchers will often be interested in evaluating or examining these programs to find out how well they are working, which aspects to keep and which aspects to modify.

Of course, there could be a number of variations on the topic, problem, broad research question and purpose provided at the end of each of the research projects summarised above. Now you have the opportunity to suggest another broad research question for each project area.

 For your notebook

Exercise 1.3 Constructing broad research questions

Reread each of the above three examples of research projects, including the sample broad research question under each example.

Now imagine that your intention is to plan a research project in each of these areas.

Write an alternative broad research question for each research project. Keep your questions simple, short and clear.

You might also like to share your questions with a study buddy or classmate.

For your notebook

Exercise 1.4 Developing broad questions for your research ideas

Have another look at your response to Exercise 1.1. Note any similarities or differences between those initial ideas and the three research examples above. Which example resonates most closely with your ideas and in what ways are your ideas similar to or different from that example?

Now write a *broad research question* for each of your main initial ideas. Again, keep your questions simple, short and clear.

There is no need to refine your questions at this stage, but make sure that you keep copies in your notebook, as you will need these questions in Chapter 2, where you will learn about developing specific research questions from your broad research questions.

WHY YOUR RESEARCH TOPIC IS IMPORTANT

Your topic needs to matter. A small-scale research project may not be ground-breaking or change the ways in which schools operate or the way that a curriculum area is taught across the nation, but it can still matter and be important to you and to others in your particular context. Teachers (and pre-service teachers) often discuss problems that require solutions. Your research could enable you to make a contribution that is quite unique. This is because it could be the first time that someone has conducted a systematic investigation into this problem in this particular context and with this particular cohort of students. Depending on your topic, your research might help you to become a better teacher, a better teacher librarian or a better school leader, or it might help your students to become better learners. It might lead to parents becoming more engaged in their children's learning. Perhaps just as importantly, learning how to conduct a small-scale research project helps you to consider more systematically problems that you encounter in your teaching context and to seek realistic, evidence-based solutions to everyday professional concerns.

In turning the pages of your national/state/territory/ province/county or local newspaper, or listening to the news on the radio or television or following discussions on social media, you will note educational issues of current concern. You may even see or hear of reports of research being conducted in one or more of your areas of interest that you noted in Exercise 1.1. Of course, you only get glimpses of the stories or hear short summaries of the research, but it would probably be difficult to go for a whole day without hearing about an educational issue in the media, social media or even on Twitter. What you hear through the media or from discussions between or with teachers provides a rough barometer of some issues of current concern. Your research ideas might happen to resonate broadly with some of these concerns or may be much more particular to your own context. Either way, you should ask yourself why your research topic is important and for whom it is important.

 For your notebook

Exercise 1.5 Is your research idea a topic of current concern?

In your notebook, record when and where in the media, social media or elsewhere you saw or heard something about research or even just concerns about the same or similar topic to one of the ideas that you noted in Exercise 1.1. From now on, you can continue to listen and watch for media reports on topics in your areas of research interest. If reports are about research being conducted, you could make notes about whether the topic is of interest nationally or at the state/territory/province/county or local level.

You may happen to hear from these reports who the researchers are and where the research is being conducted. It is important for researchers to find out who else is conducting, or has conducted, similar research to what they are planning.

This is part of what we will deal with in Chapter 4 when we look at how our research question might arise from or be related to previous research in our area of interest. Later, when you read reports of research that is closely connected to the research that you would like to do, you will start to get a feel for *what is already known about your topic, who has conducted research in your area and how that research was conducted.* This will help you when you plan how you would like to conduct your research.

WHERE TO NEXT?

Novice researchers are often advised to have just one research question so that their research project is more likely to be manageable for them. I also take this view, and have found that a single research question has enabled hundreds of my students to develop viable and interesting ideas for small-scale research projects. Almost inevitably, though, what you think will be a small-scale project at the outset is bigger than what you anticipate. Having a single question helps to ensure that your research is small-scale.

Occasionally, however, two or more closely related questions are appropriate for a novice researcher. Drafting several questions at the outset also provides you with a choice regarding which question to use as your plans start to take shape. Two or more questions are usually only needed where you can demonstrate how the design of the study and the methods of data collection and analysis will not lead you into overload—especially given that you will need to learn new skills at each step of the way. An example is Louise's project. She had one specific research question relating to participants' perspectives on the content of her program and one specific research question relating to the delivery of her program. Both questions were investigated at the same time.

The process of developing good research questions takes time, and the questions go through a number of drafts or iterations until you get to the question or questions that will take you through the planning, implementation and reporting of your small-scale research project. In this chapter, we have not worried about whether our *broad research question* is suitable for a small-scale research project, only that it was *simple, short and clear*, rather than unclear or ambiguous. You could narrow the focus more quickly by building into your early iterations the ideas presented in the next chapter, but there can be problems later if you narrow the focus too soon. You need to think more broadly at first, because as you narrow the focus to something manageable, you will then not only likely be more convinced about the particular direction that you would like to take with your research but you will also more likely be able to see how that small piece of the puzzle fits into the bigger picture and why it is important.

When the evidence from a number of small-scale studies begins to accumulate in a particular area, collectively the findings can say much more than a single study is likely to be able to do. In this way, the findings from your small-scale project, if based on a sound research question and a way of going about your research that is credible and defensible, could make a contribution to its field as well as to your practice.

The next chapter is where most of the work about learning how to develop good, specific research questions from your broad research question takes place. It is a chapter to which you will return a number of times because, even though you may technically have a good question by the end of Chapter 2, its particular focus and wording could change as you consider ethical issues and dilemmas in Chapter 3, find out what research is already reported in your area of interest in Chapter 4, and then work on how you will design your study and work out your methods of data collection in Chapters 5 and 6, respectively.

Even if the broad research question that you take with you from this chapter to forthcoming chapters appears to be working, it is still advisable to revisit Chapter 2 as you work through the later chapters so that you can critique the effectiveness and relevance of your specific research question.

REVIEW

You now need to have another look at the research ideas and broad research questions that you jotted down while working your way through this chapter. The following concluding exercises will lead you through this process.

CONCLUDING EXERCISES

 For your notebook

Exercise 1.6 Reviewing your notes

What research topics, problems or ideas did you identify that could be of interest to you as you work your way through this book? Review your response to Exercise 1.1.

Now show your ideas to your lecturer or research supervisor, and discuss which of them fit or could fit with the requirements of your subject or course. In particular, you may need to eliminate or modify any topics that could be considered high-risk and unsuitable directions for novice researchers. Note the outcomes of your discussions here.

 For your notebook

Exercise 1.7 Taking your ideas to further iterations

Take some time to identify a few of your ideas from Exercise 1.1 and any revisions made in Exercise 1.6 that interest you the most and are deemed suitable by your lecturer or research supervisor. Re-draft your notes about each of these ideas, identifying your *broad topic* and describing your *problem* in a sentence. Write another sentence or two in the paragraph to explain *why the idea is important and to whom* it might be important. Consider *who might benefit* from your research.

For your notebook

Exercise 1.8 Your broad research questions

Under the paragraph for each idea write your *broad research question* in its current iteration. If any of your questions are not simple, then see whether you can make them simpler. If they are long, they need to be short, while still retaining their meaning. If they are not clear to you or to someone else, then try to reword them so that they are clear. The research questions should be quite broad at this stage. (Don't peep ahead to the next chapter and try to refine your questions any further just yet.)

These are not final ideas, and they are likely to be quite rough at this stage—that is fine.

CHAPTER SUMMARY

In this chapter, you took the time to:

- brainstorm some research ideas, topics and problems that you find interesting, personally relevant and appealing and from which you will later select one idea to take with you as you work through this book. You should have a few ideas in reserve until you settle on a single idea in the next chapter.

- clarify the requirements for your research task, subject or course so that you can work through the remaining chapters with your purpose in mind, remembering that your research needs to be small-scale and low-risk.

- draft broad research questions that are simple, short and clear in your area of interest, explain why your ideas are important and to whom, and consider who might benefit from your research.

- read definitions of important key terms: correlation, data, educational research, hypothesis, interview schedule or interview guide, iterative process, longitudinal studies, qualitative research, quantitative research, research participants, small-scale research project.

TAKING IT FURTHER

Example 1: Student project—evaluation of a program

If you have a particular interest in Louise Wightman's research that evaluated a program for young and prospective young parents or you would like to see how another student conducted an evaluation of a program, look up Louise's Google Scholar profile, which lists her published research output.

FURTHER READING

Bell, J. (2010), *Doing Your Research Project: A guide for first-time researchers in education, health and social sciences* (5th ed.), Maidenhead: Open University Press.
See pp. 27–31 on Selecting a topic; Getting started; and The purpose of the study.
Creswell, J.W. (2012), *Educational Research: Planning, conducting and evaluating quantitative or qualitative research* (4th ed.), Boston: Pearson Education.
See pp. 58–61 on Identifying a research problem; What is a research problem and why is it important?; and How does the research problem differ from other parts of the research?

Further reading related to refining and evaluating specific research questions can be found at the end of Chapter 2, as that chapter goes into more depth regarding research questions.

2

More about research questions

___

This chapter will help you to:

 refine your chosen research topic, statement of the problem, broad research question and purpose of your small-scale study

 develop and refine specific research questions for your project using the framework provided.

Developing ideas about topics, problems and broad research questions that interest you as possible areas to pursue in a small-scale study places you in an ideal position to learn about how to construct specific research questions to take you through the planning of your study. This early thinking is useful for the following reasons:

- Brainstorming a range of ideas enables you to choose one idea that is likely to sustain your interest throughout the planning, implementation and reporting phases of your small-scale research project.

- Learning about the process for developing research questions is more meaningful if you have a particular focus and context in mind.

- You will then have one or perhaps a few research questions to guide your literature review.

Completing a literature review (Chapter 4) will help you to find out and take account of what is already known in your area of interest as you refine your research questions further. This work is important because you will need to be able to argue how the focus of your study and your research questions together have the potential to advance knowledge in your area of interest. Working through this chapter will help you to gain skills in research question construction and refinement that will underpin this later work. These skills will also be useful if you need to refine your specific research questions later—for example, when deciding on a suitable design for your study (Chapter 5) and the methods that you will use to collect or generate your data (Chapter 6).

In this chapter, you have the opportunity to continue to write in your notebook. The chapter has two main foci:

- First, you will revisit ideas for your small-scale research project that you thought about while working through Chapter 1, choosing one idea to pursue further and keeping another idea in reserve in case you need it later. You will interrogate these ideas more deeply to ensure that they are *clear* and that the different parts (the topic, research problem, broad research question and purpose of your research) fit together neatly and are *consistent* with each other.

- Second, you will engage with a *framework* to develop one or more specific research questions for your small-scale research project. To illustrate elements in the framework, we will draw on Louise's research, introduced in Chapter 1, which focused on the evaluation of a program that she developed and delivered with her colleagues. You will then use the framework to develop, evaluate and refine your specific questions and take them to further iterations if needed. It is here that you also have the opportunity to consider a few potential ethical issues or dilemmas raised earlier in the chapter. You can also take these thoughts with you when you proceed to Chapter 3, where possible ethical issues and dilemmas are a main focus.

CHOOSING YOUR RESEARCH TOPIC

It is now time to decide which of your ideas for a research project that you brainstormed in Chapter 1 will be the one that you pursue. It is helpful to keep at least one additional idea in reserve as you work through this chapter and even into the next chapter.

 For your notebook

Exercise 2.1 Choosing your research topic, broad research question and associated statements

Return to your notes from Exercise 1.7 in Chapter 1. After reviewing your notes, select one research topic and associated explanation of the problem, broad research question, statement about the purpose of your research and notes about why your idea is important and to whom, as well as who might benefit from your research.

Choose a second area to keep in reserve in case you change your mind later.

Ensure that your choice of topic is relevant to your studies and also puzzles or excites you, makes you curious or challenges you. This approach will save time and help to maintain your motivation.

Label your response 'Exercise 2.1 Choosing your research topic, broad research question and associated statements' for ease of cross-referencing later.

REFINING YOUR IDEAS: CLARITY

The following exercise for your notebook will help you to check and refine your ideas for your research project and to ensure that they are clear.

 For your notebook

Exercise 2.2 Clarity of topic, broad research question and accompanying statements

Use the following criteria to examine your chosen research topic, explanation of the problem, broad research question, purpose statement and statements about why the research is important and to whom, and who might benefit from the research, to check for *clarity*. Make refinements as needed.

Clarity means:

- using commonly understood language and terminology

- using direct language and removing excess wordage (although not to the extent that some assumptions remain in your head without being transferred to the page)

- using correct grammar and syntax (arrangement of the words)

- writing any acronyms out in full the first time (with the acronym in parentheses after the words)

- ensuring that the research topic, explanation of the problem, purpose statement and statements about why the research is important and to whom, and who might benefit from the research, do not contain questions or question marks (to distinguish them from the broad research question)

- ensuring that the broad research question is a question rather than a statement and has a question mark.

Label your response 'Exercise 2.2 Clarity of topic, broad research question and accompanying statements'.

REFINING YOUR IDEAS: CONSISTENCY

Checking for *consistency* means looking at the alignment between the research topic, the explanation of the problem, the broad research question and the accompanying statements about the purpose of your research, why it is important and to whom, and who might benefit from your research. There needs to be a *basic, internal logic* connecting all parts such that it is feasible that each part can be seen to connect to the other parts or could arise from them.

The following exercise will help you to examine what is meant by consistency between these parts by looking more closely at the examples of research provided in Chapter 1 before examining your own ideas about consistency.

For your notebook

Exercise 2.3 Consistency between the parts

Return to the three examples of research projects introduced in Chapter 1, this time with the purpose of looking for *consistency* between the description of the project, research topic, explanation of the problem, broad research question and purpose statement for each example.

Imagine that the points for each example were on separate cards and that the cards from the three projects were combined and rearranged in random order. If there is a *consistency* or *internal logic* within each project, then it should not be difficult to put everything back together again — particularly as the research projects are quite different from each other. There should be consistency across the different parts within each project, meaning that each point is logically related to the other points, even though some of the choices made may not be the only possibilities.

You might even see where you would make refinements or changes if you were the researcher taking these ideas to next iterations. As research topics and broad research questions in particular are written at more general rather than specific levels, it is likely that there will be a number of possible options.

Note who you think might be most interested in these research projects and for whom the research might be of most benefit.

Now return to your chosen research topic, broad research question and accompanying statements, checking for consistency between these parts and making adjustments as needed. Ensure that you record in your notebook for Exercise 2.3 your full response for these parts of your chosen work for later reference and before proceeding to the next exercise to see what other people think.

CLARITY AND CONSISTENCY BETWEEN THE PARTS: WHAT DO OTHERS THINK?

Taking opportunities to get other people to look at your ideas during the early stages of your thinking can be very valuable. If others are unsure of what you mean or how your ideas relate to each other, then you can make the necessary refinements and get all of your ducks in a row before proceeding further. The following exercise works well on a one-to-one basis or with several people in a group. It is a technique that you will use again later—for example, in Chapter 6, where you will be working on developing your instruments (such as interview guides or interview schedules or surveys) to collect data for your study.

 For your notebook

Exercise 2.4 Research topic, broad research question and accompanying statements: What do others think about the clarity and consistency?

Give copies of your chosen research topic, explanation of the problem, broad research question, purpose statement and statements about why the research is important and to whom, and who might benefit from the research, to several other people to read individually for clarity.

- Have each person explain to the group what he or she *understood* by your research topic, explanation of the problem, broad research question and accompanying statements.

- Discuss any differences in interpretations with the group and explain what you meant by any parts of your work that were unclear.

- Encourage interaction between the members of the group about how to improve the clarity of the individual parts of your work.

- Repeat the above steps focusing on *consistency* between the parts of your ideas.

- If you made refinements to your work while completing this exercise, you may like to show your refined ideas to one or two other people who have not yet seen your work and ask them to check your ideas for clarity and consistency.

Record the latest iteration of your work as 'Exercise 2.4 Research topic, broad research question and accompanying statements: What do others think about the clarity and consistency?'

Now that you have chosen your topic, checked your ideas for clarity and consistency, and made any necessary refinements, we now move to the second part of the chapter, which will lead you through a process for developing, evaluating and refining specific research questions. You will use these specific research questions as you move forward with planning your small-scale research project in later chapters.

FRAMEWORK FOR DEVELOPING, EVALUATING AND REFINING SPECIFIC RESEARCH QUESTIONS

When developing ideas for your project, you may see that a range of specific research questions could fit under your broad research question. You make your final choice for your specific research question/s from among these possibilities, taking into account your ideas about the intended *purpose* of your research and what you think that you could accomplish as a single, novice researcher in the amount of time available to you. It can be quite difficult to convey all the relevant information in a specific research question, and researchers can often spend a lot of time revising their initial and later draft questions.

Narrowing the broad research question to develop specific research questions requires taking a small part of the bigger picture, which is often achieved by thinking about a *specific context* in which the research could be conducted and considering who the *participants* in the research might be. This is where your thinking about your current, future or anticipated work context could be very helpful. You may even think about a context in which you were or are involved as part of your practical placement in a school. You do not (and probably should not) identify this particular context in your writing, but it can be helpful to keep a mental picture of that context in your mind as you consider the options available to you and proceed with your thinking and your plans. Of course, this can be difficult when writing research questions to fit with contexts that are currently unknown to you, such as the location of your next professional practice placement where your research may be conducted.

When planning her small-scale research project, Louise thought about her context and who her participants could be. We have already established the following about Louise's research:

- *Broad topic:* Community education programs for young parents.
- *Problem:* Making decisions around the content and delivery of education programs to meet the needs of young and prospective young parents.
- *Broad research question:* What do young and prospective

young parents look for in community education programs designed to help them adjust to parenthood?

- *Purpose:* To identify from the perspectives of participants in an education program for young parents strengths and areas for further enhancement in the content and delivery of the program that she designed.

Louise reported that her program was delivered in weekly sessions over twelve consecutive weeks to new groups of young and prospective young parents four times successively across the year. This means that Louise could potentially invite parents from one or more of these groups to be participants in her research. These possibilities gave her a number of options when it came to deciding on the particular focus of her study and her specific research questions. For example, she may have been interested to know whether the parents in the different groups had similar views about what they perceived to be strengths in the content that was covered in the program, whether young parents and prospective young parents had different needs or whether the age of their babies made any difference to what they needed to know. These groups may also have had similar or different views about the delivery of the program, such as the total length of the program and the length of the weekly sessions. Many other points around content and delivery may also have been important, so what initially seemed a simple and straightforward project was perhaps more complex than Louise first envisaged. Taking the time to brainstorm the range of possibilities may produce a large and confusing number of possibilities, but thinking about the *context* and also about the *requirements of her study* helped Louise to make her final decisions and to develop specific research questions around those decisions.

Another purpose for Louise could have been to find out from young parents who did not participate in such a program what content they thought it most relevant to include and how they thought that such programs could best be delivered. In her *context*, however, Louise had access only to successive groups of young and prospective young parents who undertook the program that she designed. Both young mothers and young fathers attended the program, although the attendance of the fathers was more ad hoc. To keep her research project *small-scale and manageable*, Louise decided to invite just eight young mothers from the fifteen who attended any of the single deliveries of the program across the year to take part in her research, and to limit her data collection to a six-week window that fitted in with her timeframe and the requirements of her studies. As she developed her *specific research questions*, she thought of her research as a **preliminary project** and appreciated that if other groups had been involved, they may have raised additional points for her to consider in refining her program.

Louise also needed to consider not only the fact that she was a *novice researcher* who would need to learn new skills but also how much time she had available to plan and implement her small-scale study and to report the findings. She decided that focusing on a **sample** of just one group would not only enable her to spend the time to explore participants' ideas more deeply but also to collect and analyse her data and to write her research

Preliminary (or pilot) project Being small in scale and often limited to relatively few participants, this can be a good starting point for novice researchers. If the opportunity arises, the researcher can build on this valuable experience and extend the participant base in later phases of the study.

Sample A sub-section of the population of people who fit into a particular category.

report within one semester, having completed the literature review and planned her study during the previous semester. It is also worth noting that novice researchers are often advised to focus on research that is qualitative or quantitative only, as using **mixed-methods research** is much more demanding and often better left until researchers have more experience.

Louise was interested in just one young parents program from among all the young parents programs available. She chose to include in her small-scale study a sample of young mothers who completed her particular program in the year during which she undertook her research. Her sample was chosen for convenience, and so it was a **convenience sample**.

As Louise continued to think about her research and proceed towards developing specific research questions, she also found that there were ethical issues to consider. For example, if Louise were to explore what participants in the program thought about the skills or skill levels of the presenters rather than the content and delivery of the program, then such a change in focus would not only be at odds with the *purpose* of her research, but it might also present an *ethical issue or dilemma* that she would be wise to avoid. Instead, the *data* that she collected needed to enable her to explore what participants considered were strengths in the content and delivery of the program and how they thought these areas could be enhanced further rather than to focus on the presenters of the program or to rate their skills.

Mixed-methods research
Involves the collection of quantitative and qualitative data, which means that a wide range of skills is needed to plan, implement and report on the research. It can be more difficult to conduct mixed-methods research when the research needs to be small-scale and completed within a short timeframe.

Convenience sample
Made up of people who are easy to reach, available, convenient or close to hand.

Louise also needed to remember that her intention to explore participants' thoughts pointed to the need for the collection of *qualitative* data in the form of words from the participants. This meant that Louise would need to avoid words or terminology in her research questions that referred to measurement or implied quantification or statistics, such as correlation, which we talked about in Chapter 1, and even phrases such as 'to what extent', which also imply measurement. She would also be wise to avoid wording her research questions in such a way that they invited yes/no responses. While this approach is sometimes appropriate with quantitative research, it does not imply the type of responses required when researchers wish to explore an area in depth using qualitative methods such as interviews. Thus it is important to consider how the *words or phrases used in specific research questions* need to take account of the *type of data to be collected* (qualitative or quantitative) and *ethical issues* that could potentially present dilemmas for the researcher.

This process involved Louise in thinking about what could be most important to know, how her research would matter (to someone) and how it could *inform her practice*. She needed to consider whose perspectives were of most interest. The last thing that she wanted to do was to have participants evaluate the presenters, especially her colleagues.

One potential area of concern that did not present itself for Louise, but can be present when teachers conduct research involving their students, is power relationships. Teachers need to be aware that these relationships can affect the responses provided to them by their students or even whether their students are willing to participate in the research. While teachers or pre-service teachers may not perceive any coercion, students may feel coerced. Teachers therefore need to be alert to this possibility when planning and conducting research involving their students, and think ahead to ethical issues that could later present as dilemmas.

Finally, Louise decided that the focus of the evaluation would be on two aspects: the content and the delivery of the program, both from the perspectives of the program participants alone. This would give her a clear and ethical focus and keep the research *within her capability*, given not just her position as a novice researcher but the busy context of her other studies and her life circumstances. By not also including the perspectives of the facilitators delivering the program, however, she was unable to identify and explore how the perspectives of the participants and the facilitators in the program complemented each other, were similar or were different. For example, the facilitators may have been able to identify other content that young and prospective young parents might need that young parents themselves may not have been able to anticipate or articulate. Thus exploring the perspectives of both groups could provide a more informed response. All research has its limitations, however, and it is important to be realistic about what can be achieved— although it is also important to acknowledge limitations such as these when you write your research report.

A word of warning

Imagine, for example, that you become aware of or develop a new way of teaching spelling to children who have difficulty with spelling and would like to compare an existing approach and the new approach. Perhaps one of the ideas that you consider is to place half of the children who have difficulty with spelling (for example, at Year 3 level at your school) in one classroom where the teacher uses your new method and the other half of the children into a classroom where the teacher uses an existing method. You design your study around comparing the two methods. There are many things to take into account and a number of variations on this general approach, but perhaps one of the main considerations is that you may not have the capacity in your position within the school to disrupt the way that the students are distributed or redistributed into different classes.

Even if the principal of the school thought that there could be merit in the idea, he or she might be reluctant for many reasons to consider allowing the research to proceed in that way. It is not just what you want to find out that is important *but who would be impacted by the research* (in this case, all of the Year 3 teachers and students in the school) and who might have a vested interest, such as parents who for various reasons may not agree to the changes in class composition and the possibility of a change of teacher for that subject. They may also be concerned about their children being singled out as poor spellers. The idea for the research may seem good at first, but could be outweighed by ethical issues and issues around the capacity of the researcher to effect the changes proposed. Research such as this would be considered a type of experiment, and it illustrates how experimental research may not always be appropriate in educational settings. It may just mean that the researcher needs to think of a range of possible ways that the research could be conducted and what it might be realistic to do and to achieve. The researcher would think about these points when developing the specific research questions.

We are starting to see that there are likely to be choices in the *purpose* of a particular piece of research and who might be *participants* in the research. At this early stage of planning your research, you might place several options on the table, even though you may have a particular preference. In Chapter 4, where you search for and critique **evidence-based research articles** in your area of interest, your aim will be to find out what is already known about your topic and how it is known (how previous research in the area was conducted).

You will also revisit your earlier ideas and possibly make adjustments to take account of existing knowledge. For example, you may wish to replicate a small-scale study in your area of interest in a different context, or perhaps a different subject or year level so that you can compare the findings from your research with the findings of earlier studies. If you were Louise, you might decide to do just that or you might decide to explore the perspectives of a different group of people, such as professionals who regularly work with prospective mothers and are aware of common gaps in their understanding or knowledge. By examining previous research in our area of interest, therefore, we are able to plan small-scale studies that complement what is already known.

In summary, drawing on the points above and previous discussion, we can see that Louise's *specific research questions* for her small-scale project need to take account of:

Evidence-based research articles Typically found in academic journals, and include a title, abstract (summary of the research), critical review of previous research in the area, methods section detailing how the study was conducted, results and/ or findings section based on analysis of the data collected or generated, discussion section and conclusions about where the research could go next or how the findings could be relevant to practitioners, and a reference list.

- the intended purpose of her research (which needs to be consistent with her topic, problem and broad research question)

- course requirements, timeframe, time available and capacity as a novice researcher
- the context in which the research will be conducted
- participants or participant groups of interest to her (her sample)
- those to whom her research would matter and how it could inform her practice
- the type of data (qualitative or quantitative) needed for her research focus, and words and phrases that point to the type of data to be collected
- how the research questions need to be simple, not too long, clear and easily understood
- possible ethical issues and dilemmas
- how the specific research questions relate to each other (if there is more than one)
- previous research (as reported in evidence-based research articles).

All the above points, apart from the last one, which depends on the outcomes of a literature review, can now be taken into account when evaluating the specific research questions for Louise's small-scale study. You will then use the same framework to draft specific research questions related to your own research ideas, to evaluate them and to take them to later iterations.

APPLYING THE FRAMEWORK TO LOUISE'S SPECIFIC RESEARCH QUESTIONS

Louise developed the following two specific research questions around her topic, the statement of her problem, her broad research question and the purpose of her study:

- How effective was the content of the Young Parents Program in meeting the needs of the participants?
- How effective did the participants in the Young Parents Program find the delivery of the program?

Table 2.1 lists the ten elements in the framework for developing, evaluating and refining specific research questions and provides brief notes explaining how Louise's specific research questions took account of the elements.

Table 2.1 Louise's specific research questions and how they address the framework

Elements in the framework for developing, evaluating and refining specific research questions	Specific research question 1	Specific research question 2
	How effective was the content of the Young Parents Program in meeting the needs of the participants?	How effective did the participants in the Young Parents Program find the delivery of the program?
1 Broad topic, problem, broad research question, purpose	**Broad topic:** Community education programs for young parents **Problem:** Making decisions around the content and delivery of education programs to meet the needs of young and prospective young parents **Broad research question:** What do young and prospective young parents look for in community education programs designed to help them adjust to parenthood? **Purpose:** To identify from the perspectives of participants in an education program for young parents strengths and areas for further enhancement in the content and delivery of the program	

Elements in the framework for developing, evaluating and refining specific research questions	Specific research question 1	Specific research question 2
	How effective was the content of the Young Parents Program in meeting the needs of the participants?	How effective did the participants in the Young Parents Program find the delivery of the program?
2 Course requirements, timeframe, time available, capacity as a novice researcher	The course required the implementation and reporting of a previously planned small-scale project to be completed within one semester. Six weeks for data collection (surveys and a focus group interview) was reasonable for accessing participants and completing all of the requirements for a first-time researcher.	
3 Context for the research	Louise was able to undertake her research in her work environment.	
4 Participants or participant groups of interest (sample)	As Louise was evaluating a program that she designed (and delivered, together with her colleagues) it was logical to involve in the research a sample of young and prospective young mothers who participated in the program. Louise did not wish at that stage to focus on the perceptions of others, such as the people who delivered the program. Her focus needed to be narrow enough to be feasible. Both specific research questions mention participants of the program of interest to Louise. Perhaps the research questions could have been more specific and referred to mothers, as Louise decided that it was the mothers, rather than the fathers, who were her focus for the study.	

Elements in the framework for developing, evaluating and refining specific research questions	Specific research question 1	Specific research question 2
	How effective was the content of the Young Parents Program in meeting the needs of the participants?	How effective did the participants in the Young Parents Program find the delivery of the program?
5 To whom the research would matter and how it could inform practice	The findings from the study mattered to Louise and to her colleagues. This was because the findings had the potential to inform aspects of the content and delivery of the program in order to retain what participants regarded as strengths and to enhance the content and delivery of the program for future cohorts of young mothers and prospective young mothers.	
6 Type of data (qualitative or quantitative) needed	Louise decided that she wanted to explore what the participants thought, so the wording of her specific research questions needed to be consistent with a qualitative study and to avoid words like 'correlation' or phrases such as 'to what extent', which both imply quantification and measurement.	
7 Simple, not too long, clear and easily understood research questions	The two specific research questions have similar wording, with the differences reflecting the focus on the *content* of the program for the first question and the *delivery* for the second question. They appear to be simple, clear and easily understood, but you may have a different view and could even suggest alterations to the wording that would make the questions better in these regards and still consistent with the focus of the study.	
8 Possible ethical issues and dilemmas	The specific research questions avoid asking the participants to critique or rate the skills of those presenting the program, which is consistent with avoiding a possible ethical issue or dilemma identified earlier.	

Elements in the framework for developing, evaluating and refining specific research questions	Specific research question 1	Specific research question 2
	How effective was the content of the Young Parents Program in meeting the needs of the participants?	How effective did the participants in the Young Parents Program find the delivery of the program?
9 How the specific research questions relate to each other	The specific research questions relate to different but complementary aspects of the program, with one focusing on the content and the other on the delivery of that content. While it appears that the questions can be explored separately, there is probably also some connection between them. For example, some participants in the study may feel that some content is better delivered in one way and other content in a different way. Qualitative surveys and the opportunity to interview participants in a group where they can interact with each other perhaps provide a good opportunity for connections like these to be identified and explored.	
10 Previous research	Even though it is not evident from our discussion so far because we deal with critiquing relevant research reports in a literature review in Chapter 4, Louise shows in her published report of her research how her study was connected to previous research. Later you can read one of her research reports where these connections are made. It will only be at that stage that you will also be able to ensure that your specific research questions are connected to previous research in your area.	

DEVELOPING FIRST ITERATIONS OF YOUR SPECIFIC RESEARCH QUESTIONS

After working your way through the notes in Table 2.1 and thinking about how Louise's specific research questions took account of the elements in the framework, it is now time for you to draft one or two specific research questions relating to the ideas that you recorded as Exercise 2.1 in your notebook.

 For your notebook

Exercise 2.5 First iteration of your specific research question/s

Returning to your ideas from Exercise 2.1 relating to your chosen research topic, broad research question and associated statements, think further about your developing research ideas and draft one or two specific research questions to guide your small-scale study.

Remember that the questions are drafts only and will undergo further iterations later. In your notebook, draw up a table like Table 2.2 to record your draft specific research question/s and to make notes about how your question/s take account of the first nine elements from the framework, similar to Table 2.1 above. You will be able to revise your ideas and complete your notes on the final element later, after working your way through Chapter 4.

Table 2.2 Your specific research questions and how they address the framework

Elements in the framework for developing, evaluating and refining specific research questions	Specific research question 1	Specific research question 2 (if required)
1 Broad topic, problem, broad research question, purpose	Broad topic: Problem: Broad research question: Purpose:	
2 Course requirements, timeframe, time available, capacity as a novice researcher		
3 Context for the research		
4 Participants or participant groups of interest (sample)		
5 To whom the research would matter and how it could inform practice		

Elements in the framework for developing, evaluating and refining specific research questions	Specific research question 1	Specific research question 2 (if required)
6 Type of data (qualitative or quantitative) needed		
7 Simple, not too long, clear and easily understood research questions		
8 Possible ethical issues and dilemmas		
9 How the specific research questions relate to each other		
10 Previous research		

Even though you have begun to refine your initial ideas and to take them to further iterations, all ideas are still quite tentative at this stage. Further refinements will be considered later as you work through Chapter 4, where you search for and locate evidence-based research articles relating to research already conducted in your area of interest, and find out what is already known and what questions still need exploring or investigating. You may still retain your general area of interest but modify some of the developing detail as you read and think further.

CHAPTER SUMMARY

In this chapter, you took the time to:

- narrow down from among your list of possibilities for a research project from Chapter 1 (Exercise 1.7) your choice of one topic, broad research question and accompanying statements to proceed with in this chapter and beyond, keeping one of your other ideas 'in reserve'

- refine your ideas by checking for clarity and consistency across your chosen topic, broad research question and accompanying statements and consistency between these parts

- draft broad research questions that are simple, short and clear in your area of interest

- draft the first iteration of your specific research question/s and make notes on how your question takes account of the first nine elements from the framework provided

- read definitions of important key terms: convenience sample, evidence-based research articles, mixed-methods research, preliminary (or pilot) project, sample.

FURTHER READING

Lambert, M. (2012), *A Beginner's Guide to Doing Your Education Research Project*, London: Sage.

See pp. 65–78 on: What are research questions?; What makes 'good' research questions?; Where to start?; A suggested framework; Other kinds of research questions; Some further characteristics; Thinking about the project as a whole; Development; Looking ahead.

3
Ethics

This chapter will help you to:

 consider ethical issues and dilemmas at each stage in the research process

 identify the ethical issues and dilemmas associated with your research and procedures for seeking ethical clearance.

Ethical issues and dilemmas are present at each stage of the research process, from planning the research project to the practicalities of conducting the research through to interpreting the data, reporting the findings and making recommendations for future research and practice. How an ethical issue or dilemma is handled in the early stages of planning the research project, even when drafting research questions, can have implications for the practicalities of conducting and reporting the research as well as beyond the life of the project.

Consideration of ethical issues has come a long way and, while some past practices are not acceptable today, other challenges are creeping into view. Here are a few examples.

- In scientific or medical research, due diligence is required so that researchers remain sensitised to the feelings, perspectives and rights of individuals as new frontiers are broken before the full range of ethical implications can be realised, debated and taken into account.
- Rapid advances in social media and their use in everyday life leave behind a trail of images (often of vulnerable persons) that cannot be deleted and are taken without the consent or knowledge of those whose images are portrayed.
- Observation of people and their actions is now quite ubiquitous, through devices such as closed-circuit television (CCT) cameras, the ability to record telephone conversations and surveillance of online spaces.

Debates around safety and protection, no harm intended and apparent social acceptance of monitoring of people and their actions, respectively, may occur in the context of the above examples. When considering these types of ethical issues or dilemmas and others as relevant to your research project, however, thinking needs to be deep, systematic, protracted across the life of the project and cognisant of the perspectives of research participants as well as others who are impacted by your research.

This chapter provides an opportunity before your project commences to pause and to begin to think deeply about *ethical issues and dilemmas* related to the *planning, conduct and reporting* of your research. Researchers need to do everything in their power to anticipate, minimise and possibly circumvent ethically problematic situations that could arise during their research. This includes research involving both adults and children. Even so, there will almost certainly be issues and dilemmas that cannot be anticipated, and that will need to be dealt with as they arise. Guillemin and Gillam (2004) refer to this undertaking as **ethics in practice,** and argue that **reflexivity,** or the ongoing critical reflection proposed above, is an essential tool for researchers to practise during each phase of the study.

Our discussion around ethical issues and dilemmas related to planning, conducting and reporting research focuses primarily on principles of *anonymity, confidentiality, avoidance of harm* and the *rights and protection* of participants and researcher in small-scale research projects. It is important to begin to engage in discussions and debates around these principles before turning your attention to applying for ethical clearance to conduct research, a process referred to by Guillemin and Gillam (2004) as **procedural ethics.** The final discussion in the chapter is devoted to applying for ethical clearance to conduct your study.

Ethics in practice Refers to the ethical considerations that arise during the conduct of research and that require the researcher's attention at the time.

Reflexivity Ongoing reflection on ethical issues and dilemmas, which needs to occur throughout the life of the project, from the planning through to implementation and reporting of the research.

Procedural ethics Involves the preparation and submission of formal ethics applications to conduct research. The research must not commence unless and until notification is received that the application for ethical clearance has been approved.

Before continuing, it is really important to note that *under no circumstances* should your research commence or any data be collected or generated before applications for ethical clearance are submitted *and* official approval from the relevant ethics committees is given for the research to be undertaken.

ETHICAL ISSUES AND DILEMMAS: PLANNING AND CONDUCTING YOUR SMALL-SCALE RESEARCH PROJECT

This section of the chapter has two main foci. First, it takes into account ethical considerations around the choice of research topic, raising some important points to discuss with your lecturer. Second, it looks more specifically at ethical issues and dilemmas around anonymity and confidentiality, the avoidance of harm, and the rights and protection of participants and researcher in planning and conducting your research.

Ethical considerations around choice of topic

Consideration of ethical issues commences with deciding the topic of your research. Some topics would be too 'hot' to handle and obviously outside of your area of expertise or the brief given to you in your course or subject. Occasionally, students may find in the list of topics they brainstormed initially, that some ideas which appeared fine on the surface had unexpected implications, and discussions with their lecturer or research supervisor led them to other topics. Novice researchers are on steep learning curves at each stage of their research, and it makes sense to keep the research as uncomplicated as possible, avoiding topics or situations about which the research supervisor or lecturer has concerns. The research questions, both broad and specific, reflect the focus of the topic.

If your topic (and therefore your research) focuses on children, then it is important to remember that the same ethical considerations that are relevant for adults are also relevant for children. Morrow and Richards (1996) note three further considerations that need to be taken into account when children are intended participants in research:

children's competence or capacity to provide informed consent to participate in the research (or to decide not to participate) and the importance of gatekeepers when seeking consent; the responsibilities of researchers to consider the vulnerability of children; and the power the researcher exercises when interpreting and analysing data from children. These considerations need to be discussed with your lecturer or research supervisor when thinking about your topic as well as at the later stages of the research process.

It is still important to select a topic about which you are passionate or curious, one that challenges or excites you. There are times when one of the topics being considered could be close to home. Perhaps the student has a long-held desire to research a particular topic—for example, the education of children with disabilities—but it is the particular angle and perspective taken that often needs more careful deliberation together with the other considerations mentioned above. We need to have deep conversations about the sensitivity of the topic and children's competencies and vulnerability when choosing our topic and our methods for seeking consent if we are planning research that involves children.

A helpful point to remember is that your first, small-scale project is unlikely to be conducted for the purpose of making ground-breaking discoveries or reaching conclusions that will change the way that an area within education is funded or approached across the country. Instead, it is often the case that the research will leave you with more questions about your area of interest and these questions could replace assumptions that you may previously considered to be foregone conclusions. Research often opens up a complexity that students did not know existed. It helps students to think differently about the problems and challenges that caught their interest and it helps them to learn to think more systematically about those and other problems and challenges that they face professionally. While choosing a topic that makes us curious is still important, the particular topic that we choose from among those that interest us is less important than the safety, rights and protection of our participants and those around them.

Safety, rights and protection of participants and others

Let us assume that you have discussed your topic with your research supervisor or lecturer, your topic is at least tentatively accepted, and your broad and specific research questions and statements about the purpose of your study, why your research is important and for whom are all in alignment. We will now consider ethical issues and possible dilemmas around *anonymity and confidentiality*, the *avoidance of harm* and the *rights and protection* of your participants as well as yourself in planning the details of your project and in conducting your research.

Anonymity and confidentiality are quite complex, interrelated concepts. It is often not possible to be able to guarantee that you can adhere to both throughout all stages of the research, and so they need to be considered at each step. At one level, **anonymity** means that the participant's identity is unknown or at least not revealed. **Confidentiality** means that what participants communicate with you or what you find out during the data collection will not be revealed to others except as agreed in advance. It may not be possible to guarantee anonymity at all stages, although it is usually maintained

Anonymity Not revealing the identities of the participants in your research.

Confidentiality Closely related to anonymity. Selected data in the form of words are often used in the research report, although to maintain confidentiality, participants' words are usually presented anonymously or using pseudonyms, unless there is prior agreement.

when the research is reported. Researchers need to consider what they can promise and they need to honour their promises.

It is important to consider carefully the questions that you plan to ask on surveys and in interviews, and to think about what you might note when making observations, not just in terms of what you need to find out in order to answer your research questions but *what, how and when you ask and in whose company* (such as in group interviews or focus group interviews). Interviewing children or members of other vulnerable groups—including some groups of adults—can carry higher levels of risk than interviewing adults who are not members of vulnerable groups. It will be important to reflect deeply and have conversations around whether it is better to interview children in groups or individually, and where interviews should be held. For example, you may consider that children will feel more comfortable with group interviews, particularly if the researcher is unknown to them, but this is not a foregone conclusion. The *safety and welfare* of all involved is a complex area that needs careful consideration.

Data-collection instruments Used to collect data from the participants in a study. They may include surveys or questionnaires, achievement tests, interview schedules or interview guides and observation schedules.

Even though you will think about *ethical issues* and possible *dilemmas* while constructing your **data-collection instruments**, stopping to think specifically about ethical issues provides an opportunity to scrutinise your instruments again. Particularly important is thinking from the participants' perspectives and imagining that you are in their position. Using a philosophical approach, you can imagine scenarios and consider not just why you should ask your questions but also think deeply about what you ask, how, when and in whose company.

You should discuss with your research supervisor or lecturer the questions that you plan to ask. Sometimes you may face a dilemma about whether to ask a question or how to phrase it—for example, if the question is key to your research question yet could seem a little invasive. This might be a time to look more closely at your topic. Without even being aware of it, you could have a participant in witness protection or some who will be in danger if their identity or whereabouts is revealed. Photographic images and what you do with them if you seek them is particularly important. It is also important to be aware of school procedures and protocols around children in this respect, as these procedures and protocols need to be followed and may, in fact, confirm that it would be wise to avoid taking images. The vulnerability of children and their parents' requests must be respected at all times.

Researchers will often ask whether they can audio record and transcribe interviews in order to aid the collection and analysis of data. Doing your own transcripts is not only an opportunity to commence the data analysis, as you can note points related to the analysis as they occur to you at the same time, but it is imperative to *respect your participants* and *honour the agreements* that you have made with them. You might show the transcripts to those who spoke so that they can confirm whether they are still happy to have their words used for the research and they can take the opportunity to clarify points that they think, on reflection, could otherwise be misunderstood. I advise all novice researchers to complete their own transcripts, even though it is time-consuming to do so, because of the *opportunities for learning* and *initial data analysis*. You may also consider this to be an ethical choice made out of *respect for your participants*, who may not be comfortable with another person being privy to the recordings.

During the planning stage of the research and once approval is received to conduct the research, you may need to know the identity of your participants—particularly in small-scale research in which you plan to interview people. Knowing identities may result from the way that you select your sample and whether, for example, you are seeking the involvement of people with particular characteristics that may narrow down the possibilities, especially if you plan to conduct your research at a location near to you, or where you know the people who work or study at that location. Depending on what you want to find out, this familiarity could make you and the participants feel more comfortable. It is also important to consider whether it may make the participants feel less comfortable. A consideration for you could also relate to whether you are a practising teacher researching your own practice or a pre-service teacher undertaking a practical experience. Existing or newly formed relationships in either of these situations are points for further discussion with your lecturer or research supervisor.

We cannot and should not make assumptions about whether participants may feel more or less comfortable in responding (in writing, orally or both) with someone whom they know or someone whom they did not previously know. There may be circumstances about which you are unaware that could affect the comfort levels of potential participants and their willingness to be involved in the research, and we need to *respect privacy*. While participants do not need to reveal these circumstances or their reasons for not wanting to be involved, they need to know enough about the research (including around anonymity and confidentiality) to be able to make an informed decision about whether they will participate, unless they already know that they do not wish to participate or feel unable to do so. Potential participants may also need to ask further questions about the research before they are able to decide whether they will participate. As indicated earlier, there are additional points to consider in research involving children.

If you plan to use **triangulation**, it is often necessary to record the data from participants in such a way that their responses on a survey and at an interview, for example, can be cross-referenced. Even if you decide to interview a small number of people who completed a survey and you choose your interviewees based on their responses to the survey items, you will need to know the identities of the people who complete the surveys and how they can be contacted should you wish to invite some participants to interview. The participants often cannot be *anonymous* to the researcher conducting and collecting the data, particularly in small-scale research, so care needs to be taken not to promise or guarantee anonymity beyond what is possible.

Triangulation Involves using more than one method of data collection to answer the research question/s. All methods have their strengths and limitations, so using more than one quantitative or qualitative method or using mixed methods can often help to gain a more complete answer. One method may be more dominant or they could be equally complementary.

Anonymity is also not possible when group interviews or focus group interviews are held, because the participants will be involved at the same time and in the presence of each other. Often the participants will already know each other or know of each other, and names are likely to be used during the exchange of ideas. What participants hear from each other, however, should remain *confidential*. While you cannot be completely sure that participants will keep confidence, they may need to be made aware of the importance of this expectation for the protection of others as well as themselves.

It is another part of your *respect for the participants* and for respect to be mutually present among the participants in a group or focus group interview.

It is also incumbent upon the researcher not to discuss the identities of the participants with other parties, and what participants say should also remain confidential when the data are collected. For example, when you arrive home in the evening it is important not to discuss details with family members when they ask you about your day, regardless of whether you think they will discuss it with anyone or whether you think no one else can hear the conversation. Similarly, it is important to protect data by ensuring that it is not accessible to others in paper form, electronically, as audio or video recordings or as photographs. It is important to use password protection for electronic data and to keep everything under lock and key. If you have data in your office at work, then ensure that you lock your office when you are not there. If you share an office, ensure that your data are in locked cabinets when you are not using them and when you are not in the office. Once revealed, information cannot be retrieved, and it may only be in such circumstances that we really begin to understand issues around the *avoidance of harm* and the *rights and protection* of individuals. It is simpler to try to avoid physical harm, but we are not always privy to personal circumstances that could inadvertently lead to other types of harm for our participants, including psychological harm.

There are two circumstances in which you may need to discuss or pass on what is otherwise confidential information. First, your research supervisor or lecturer may need to be a confidante. You may not need to reveal everything, but your supervisor may be in a position to guide you when you are faced with dilemmas that you identify and dilemmas that they but not you identify. For example, the supervisor may be aware of a potential conflict of interest that is not evident unless he or she knows the location or your participants. The second circumstance is where a participant, even in passing, reveals to you information that legally you must report.

Even so, these examples illustrate the importance of constantly being alert and also of engaging in the ongoing reflexivity or reflection that Guillemin and Gillam (2004) recommend throughout the life of the project. We should not wait until unplanned things happen or something goes wrong before engaging in deep reflection on matters of ethics or when faced with ethical dilemmas and are wondering what to do. Instead, we should regularly revisit the guidelines that arise from our formal application to conduct research to ensure that we are still acting according to the approvals given, stay in communication with our lecturer or research supervisor, and think deeply on an ongoing basis about how our research is conducted and the impact that it has on participants and those around them. As noted by Guillemin and Gillam, approval from the appropriate ethics committees to conduct the research does not relieve researchers of their duties and responsibilities.

In planning their projects, researchers also need to consider the *opportunities and benefits* that their research may provide to participants or the community in which the research is to be conducted (taking care not to inflate ideas about participant opportunities or benefits). Researchers also need to consider dilemmas with which they might be faced in relation to omission. Imagine that you plan to provide one group of participants with an experience that you hypothesise will be of benefit to them and that, for purposes of comparison, you do not offer the same experience to another group. This situation may present you with a *dilemma*, and so you might think about how you could be fair to both groups. For example, depending on the situation, you could work with the teachers afterwards, as they may wish to look at the experiences that they provide to their students based on the findings from the study. If your study is a type of experiment, another option might be to discuss with your research supervisor or lecturer the advantages and disadvantages of a different type of experiment, as there are many different types.

It is not possible to solve all dilemmas, but knowing this should not be the catalyst for disbanding the conversation and your attempts to resolve the situation too early. As with nearly all decisions that you make as a researcher, a philosophical approach is paramount. Considering all sides of issues and the options, on balance, leads to final decisions that you can then argue.

ETHICAL ISSUES AND DILEMMAS: REPORTING THE RESEARCH FINDINGS

It is quite rare that the identities of participants should or will be revealed in the report of the findings of the research. Occasionally, if participants are well known and wish to have their stories told and their identities revealed, it could be appropriate to do so. An example could be if your research involves completing a biography of a leading educator. This could also involve interviewing other people, however, so each contributor to the research and each piece of information would need to be considered separately as it may not be appropriate to reveal the identities of all contributors. Research that appears simple on the surface can actually contain many issues and dilemmas. These need to be anticipated in the planning stage as much as possible, but also while the research is being conducted and when preparing the report. It is important to stop and reflect on possible ethical issues and dilemmas at key points, not just when they arise. It would be unfortunate to be dealing with a dilemma in the reporting stage when it could have been anticipated and perhaps avoided as an ethical issue much earlier.

Your small-scale study probably will not involve a biography of a person who wishes his or her identity to be revealed. Instead, it is more likely that you will need to consider using pseudonyms when reporting your findings, especially if your data are in the form of words provided by participants in writing or orally. You will most likely provide general descriptions of your participants and demographic information so that readers can make connections between your research and their circumstances, where appropriate, making your findings more meaningful and useful for them. Using pseudonyms or other ways of protecting the identities of your participants is important for the report because it is then that it is usually possible to attend to anonymity. Larger-scale quantitative research generally aggregates the data and uses statistical analyses that circumvent the need to consider pseudonyms for individual participants. As with qualitative research, however, quantitative research may use pseudonyms or provide non-identifying demographic descriptions for the sites where the research is conducted.

Reporting the findings of research carries with it the same level of responsibility as the planning and implementation stages of the study. Earlier, we mentioned how researchers can verify with their participants that they are happy to have the words that they spoke during the interview included as data. It is important to work carefully with this data and to use it wisely, so that you can show in your research report how your conclusions have been drawn faithfully from the data. More difficult can be the interpretation of data from children, which has implications for the reporting of the findings from your analysis of the data. Morrow and Richards (1996) provide sound words of advice. They remind us of the responsibilities that adults have to ensure that children are not harmed. This point extends to all stages of the research, including the reporting of the findings. Furthermore, Morrow and Richards encourage us to consider how what children tell us is affected variously by a range of attributes, such as their age and gender, as well as how they respond to adults—whether in groups or on a one-to-one basis. These considerations illustrate how ethical and reflexive practice in the planning and implementation stages of the study have implications for the findings that are reported. If your proposed research could involve children in any way at all, either directly or indirectly, then it is important to extend your reading, thinking and reflection on ethical issues and dilemmas that surround the involvement of children. The further reading at the end of this chapter will give you some starting points for your reading.

It is now time to pause and to identify possible ethical issues and dilemmas associated with your research. It is also important to take time to consider how you will deal with ethical issues around *anonymity* and *confidentiality*, how you will *protect your participants and yourself from harm* and how you will *respect the rights* of your participants.

First, it is important to step yourself through your early and developing plans for your research and to consider *ethical issues* or *dilemmas* that could arise during the planning and conduct of your research. Second, it is important to consider ethical issues and dilemmas that could arise during the reporting of your research. At present, your plans include tentative or draft ideas around your topic, broad research question and specific research questions. These ideas are subject to change as you undertake your literature review and find out what is already known on your topic or problem and how it is known (the methods used in previous research into the problem) and later as you consider other aspects of your plan.

The exercises below therefore start you on the reflexive process introduced previously. It will be important to revisit the exercises below as your plans continue to change and develop when you work through later chapters of this book. This will help to ensure that this important process can continue throughout the life of your project.

 For your notebook

Exercise 3.1 Ethical issues or dilemmas that could arise during the planning and conduct of your research

Revisit your plans for your research, including your topic, broad research question, purpose, specific research questions and other parts of your plans (as you continue to work through the book).

Carefully scrutinise each part of the plan and note possible ethical issues around the following four areas separately and in relation to each other:

- anonymity

- confidentiality

- avoidance of harm, and

- the rights and protection of participants and yourself as the researcher.

What thoughts do you have so far that could relate to each of these four areas and why do you see them as important? What points do you think that you need to weigh when thinking about your research from the perspectives of participants and yourself?

If you are further through the book and your planning:

- How did you, on balance, reach your decisions?

- What possible dilemmas are you still considering and perhaps are yet to resolve? Discuss these points with your research supervisor or lecturer.

Label your response 'Exercise 3.1 Ethical issues or dilemmas that could arise during the planning and conduct of your research' for ease of cross-referencing later.

 For your notebook

Exercise 3.2 Ethical issues or dilemmas that could arise during the reporting of your research

Look carefully at your response to Exercise 3.1.

What particular ethical issues or dilemmas could you face in reporting your research?

How are these ideas different from or similar to the issues and dilemmas that you could face in the planning and conduct of your research?

How will you handle the ethical issues and dilemmas that relate to the reporting of your research?

To facilitate your response to this exercise it would be helpful to check the requirements of your course or subject so that the issues and dilemmas that you identify and discuss take these requirements into account.

Label your response 'Exercise 3.2 Ethical issues or dilemmas that could arise during the reporting of your research'.

PROCEDURES FOR SEEKING ETHICAL CLEARANCE

Seeking ethical clearance to conduct research is both an *obligation* to which you must attend before starting your data collection and an *opportunity* to continue to think about ethical issues and dilemmas, and plan how they will be addressed.

You can work on your application for ethical clearance as your ideas for your **research proposal** grow and mature as you work through this book. It is not possible to seek ethical clearance until you know what you propose to do, but preparing your research proposal and your applications for ethical clearance to conduct your study can go hand in hand. The iterative process continues as you toggle between the two and make refinements to both sets of ideas. Data cannot be collected until your research proposal and your applications for ethical clearance to conduct the research are finalised and accepted.

Research proposal A detailed plan for your research. The exact details required can vary from one university to another but it will at least include your research questions, the purpose and justification for your study, consideration of the findings of previous research in your area, details of how you will conduct your research, a timeline, schedule of activities and proposed dates.

All research has ethical issues and dilemmas. Some may arise during the conduct of the research, even though the researcher took steps to anticipate issues and dilemmas in advance. A researcher who concludes that there are no ethical issues of concern needs to think more deeply and broadly. Such a conclusion could not be reached if we thought carefully about a range of contingencies from the point of view of the participants. Even if everything is in order and seems relatively straightforward, people do not need to participate in our research just because we ask them to do so. They also do not need to provide reasons for declining to participate or choosing to discontinue their participation.

Potential participants could also ask what the researcher will give back to the community where the researcher ideally plans to undertake the research. Some communities, such as Aboriginal or Torres Strait Islander communities, have been the focus of many research projects and the question could arise of who will actually benefit from the research. These communities would have observed a litany of promises kept or broken. They may recall the respect with which researchers approached them about their research and possibly researchers who they felt came with the expectation that the community would agree to be involved. Some researchers would have followed protocols of engagement expected by the community. Perhaps other researchers needed to do the background work first to understand the culture of the community or group and how to approach the community. This background work takes time and can impact on researchers' timelines, especially if they had not shown interest in the community and its concerns prior to expressing a desire to conduct their research. In Chapter 1, we thought about why our research is important and to whom it might be important. When thinking about ethics, these ideas can take on new meanings.

Research can only commence once the researcher gains approval. A good place to start to find out about these procedures is your university. Universities have set procedures and requirements. The research proposal and ethics application both take quite a lot of work and thinking, and may not be accepted or at least may require refinements. Researchers need to adhere strictly to the conditions attached to their approvals. While your application for ethical clearance is under consideration, you would be wise to complete or at least continue work on your literature review, which is the topic of the next chapter, as the literature review will form part of your research report, such as a chapter in a thesis or dissertation. This use of time is imperative, as you are likely to have a relatively short amount of time to complete all the work associated with planning, conducting and reporting your research.

The requirements for gaining ethics approval at universities are typically consistent with national guidelines for conducting research with humans. If the research is to be conducted in an institution such as a school, there is also the requirement to seek ethics approval from the schooling system (depending on whether one or more schools are involved) and the school. Even if ethical clearance is gained through the schooling system, the research cannot proceed unless the school and potential participants in the school also agree and prior approval has been gained through the university or faculty ethics committee. In assessing your application for ethical clearance, university ethics committees will consider the level of risk attached to your research, particularly in your capacity as a novice researcher.

Thus it may appear that seeking and gaining approval to conduct a small-scale study could involve a maze of requirements. It is important to find out the requirements for your situation and your inquiries begin with your research supervisor or lecturer. It is also important to allow plenty of time to find out what you need to do and to do it. Time needs to be built into your schedule to allow for responses to be drafted and submitted for further consideration if the initial application for ethical clearance is not approved. An early task for you is to find out to where you need to submit your ethics application. Ethics committees usually make available their meeting dates and dates by which applications need to be received in order for applications to be assessed at each meeting.

Developing a clear idea of what you want to do is important. The process is facilitated by:

- making decisions around your topic choice, broad and specific research questions, why your research is important and to whom
- working in the coming chapters on selecting your research design and methods based on your research questions and on your reading of evidence-based research in your area
- continuing to think about possible ethical issues and dilemmas while planning your study.

The process also places you in a good position to begin to prepare your research proposal and ethics applications. You will also be required to attach to your ethics applications copies of information sheets and consent forms that you will provide for your participants, possible proposed scripts for initial contact with potential participants and instruments such as interview schedules or interview guides as appropriate. You can ask about the requirements for the information sheets and consent forms, and for any other requirements, and perhaps lists of points to include and/or sample forms from your university. You can usually find information online through your institution. Your completed forms will also need to demonstrate or be underpinned by deep consideration of ethical issues and dilemmas, such as those discussed in the earlier parts of this chapter.

CONCLUSION

This chapter started by considering possible ethical issues and dilemmas that could arise during the planning, conduct and reporting of research before focusing on procedures around seeking ethical clearance. This approach was deliberate because it is difficult to work on procedures without first thinking through possible ethical issues and dilemmas with which you could be faced. Procedures should also not be the first or the main consideration, but instead need to be based on sound and sincere care for participants and their welfare. How the research is approached will depend on being able to argue for a sound proposal and methods that are underpinned by due diligence to ethical issues and dilemmas. Each research project also has its own unique set of circumstances, and possible issues and dilemmas to identify and consider.

The following concluding exercises for your notebook give you the opportunity to find out the requirements for submitting applications for ethical approval from your university and any other institution, such as a school or schooling system, where you anticipate conducting your research.

CONCLUDING EXERCISES

 For your notebook

Exercise 3.3 Requirements for ethics applications at your university

Check your course or subject outline and course notes provided by your lecturer, as well as any notes taken by you during classes or discussions with your lecturer that relate to ethics requirements and any requirements to apply for ethical approval to conduct your small-scale study if appropriate. In particular, also note due dates and timelines.

Visit any online sites suggested and contact your research supervisor or lecturer if you have any questions or wish to check requirements for your particular circumstances.

Label your response 'Exercise 3.3 Requirements for ethics applications at your university'.

 For your notebook

Exercise 3.4 Requirements for ethics applications elsewhere as appropriate

If you wish to conduct your small-scale study in a school or other institution or organisation, find out the requirements and follow through as per the previous exercise.

Check whether separate ethics applications need to go to both your university and the school or other organisation or whether, following a successful application to the organisation, the university requires you to forward the approval to them.

Label your response 'Exercise 3.4 Requirements for ethics applications elsewhere as appropriate'.

CHAPTER SUMMARY

In this chapter, you took the time to:

- think about ethical issues and dilemmas that may arise during the planning, conduct and reporting of research, with particular emphasis on anonymity, confidentiality, avoidance of harm and the rights and protection of participants and researchers

- consider these issues and dilemmas as they could apply to your small-scale research project

- find out about the requirements for seeking ethics approval from your university and other institution where you plan to conduct your study, revisiting your course requirements and notes, checking timelines for submission of applications and contacting your research supervisor or lecturer for further guidance

- read definitions of important key terms: anonymity, confidentiality, data-collection instruments, ethics in practice, procedural ethics, reflexivity, research proposal, triangulation.

FURTHER READING

Campbell, A. & Groundwater-Smith, S. (2007), *An Ethical Approach to Practitioner Research*, New York: Routledge.

Guillemin, M. & Gillam, L. (2004), Ethics, Reflexivity, and 'Ethically Important Moments' in Research, *Qualitative Inquiry*, *10*(2), pp. 261–80.

Lambert, M. (2012), *A Beginner's Guide to Doing Your Education Research Project*, London: Sage.
See pp. 21–3 on ethics and pp. 139–45 on seeking ethical approval for your project.

Morrow, V. & Richards, M. (1996), The Ethics of Social Research with Children: An overview, *Children and Society, 10,* pp. 90–105.

4
Understanding and completing a literature review

This chapter will help you to:

 locate and read evidence-based research articles and other literature relating to your topic, problem, broad research question and draft research question/s

 develop a conceptual framework, write a critical literature review and reassess your research questions.

The ideal time to start working intensively on your literature review is after you decide on a topic and a problem and learn how to draft one or two research questions in your area of interest before making decisions about your **research design** and your *methods of data collection*. Your draft research question/s will guide your search for *evidence-based research articles* on your topic and what you find out from your **literature review** will

Research design The broad approach or framework employed to investigate or explore a topic or problem and the research question. Research designs can be quantitative (for example, experiments) or qualitative, or use mixed methods (combining quantitative and qualitative). Evidence-based research articles may explicitly identify the design used in the study—for example, a case study or a longitudinal study.

Literature review The central purpose of a literature review is to find out what is already known about a specific area of interest and how we know (the design and methods used in previous studies), what still needs to be discovered and how the research builds on previous research or fits into part of a gap left by previous research. The literature review leads into the research question/s guiding the study.

help you to refine the focus of your study, your specific research question/s and how you wish to conduct your study.

The central purpose of a literature review is to find out:

- what is already known about your specific area of interest and how we know (the design and methods used in previous studies). This includes identifying the different approaches that have been used to investigate the topic of interest.
- what still needs to be discovered
- how your research builds on previous research or fits into part of a gap left by previous research.

That means that you will be able to articulate the particular contribution that your small-scale study makes to the area. Finding out how previous studies in your area were conducted, together with your knowledge of research designs (Chapter 5) and methods (Chapter 6), and your knowledge of the context in which your research will be conducted, can help you to make informed decisions about how you will conduct your study.

Sometimes the way in which a study is conducted can also add to the field. Imagine that previous quantitative research found a relationship between the year level to which teachers were assigned in their first year of teaching and level of satisfaction with career choice. The next phase of this research might be qualitative and use a different research design and methods to explore with teachers the reasons that they give for their levels of satisfaction. The long-term aim beyond a small-scale study such as yours could be to find out whether the year level to which teachers are first assigned impacts on the likelihood that they will stay in the profession longer than five years. Alternatively, the first phase of a study in this area could be the qualitative side, with a later phase extending the participant base in a quantitative study to test for a correlation between year level of first appointment and level of satisfaction with career choice. You might return to this type of thinking later when you consider the particular contribution that your small-scale study might make to your area of interest.

Your literature review, like those you will see in evidence-based research articles, is preceded by your abstract and introduction and comes before the methods section of your report, which describes how you conducted your study. A literature review also forms part of a *research proposal*, which must be written and accepted before you can proceed with your study.

If you intend to conduct research as part of your studies, there are certain requirements that must be met before you will be permitted to begin data collection. For example, you will need to plan your research, submit and/or present your research proposal, respond to questions about your proposal and make any required changes as well as satisfy requirements around ethics. Specific requirements for your research proposal will vary according to your course or subject, so it is important to check those requirements.

In preparing a literature review, the expectation is that you will:

- read quite widely in your area of interest to get a broad overview of the scope of previous research before narrowing the focus and deciding on the evidence-based research articles and other literature (if appropriate) that you will include in your review
- purposefully read and take notes on the selected articles and other literature
- draw out the themes and any debates that the literature covers, as well as the methods used to conduct previous research in your area of interest and construct a **conceptual or theoretical framework**

Conceptual or theoretical framework Consists of the themes that you drew from your reading of the reports of previous research and related literature. The literature review is shaped around these themes.

- use the conceptual or theoretical framework and your notes as a guide to structure and write a critical review of the literature. This may involve working at the descriptive level before taking your ideas and your writing to the critical level.
- take your draft research questions to later iterations as a result of your critique of the literature, or confirm that your draft research questions are suitable.

Your refined specific research questions will then guide you through the detailed planning, implementation and reporting of your study.

This chapter will take you through these steps. You will need your latest notes on your topic, problem, broad and draft specific research questions and other statements from your notebook as a guide.

IDENTIFYING, CHOOSING AND LOCATING RELEVANT LITERATURE

This section of the chapter identifies the main types of references that you might consider for inclusion in your literature review and provides practical information to help you to understand more general points that can be useful to know before you embark on locating relevant literature. It also provides suggestions for getting started with your search for literature.

Different types of references

Evidence-based research of high quality that was systematically planned and implemented is most often reported in *peer-reviewed journals* in an appropriate discipline area after going through a rigorous review process. When deciding which journals to target for their papers, researchers consider those that publish research in their area and they also consult the notes for contributors from individual journals that explain their parameters and requirements. Researchers also watch out for special issues of journals that invite reports of research in specific areas within a discipline. As you search for and read articles in your area, you will also be able to identify and compile a list of journals that publish evidence-based research articles relevant to your interest. You can then ask your university librarian how to set up electronic alerts for those journals so that you know when those journals publish articles or special issues in your area.

Other types of published articles that researchers often find informative when undertaking their own literature reviews, if they are available, are major *literature reviews* and **meta-analyses**. If you find an entire article devoted to reviewing and

Meta-analysis A review of quantitative research in a particular area. The studies reviewed need to conform to certain criteria in order to be included in the review. The aim is to be able to draw conclusions from the combination of a large number of studies in a way that is not possible using single quantitative studies alone.

critiquing the evidence-based research literature in your field of interest up to a particular date rather than reporting a single study, that article could be an important one for you to include in your review. You can then focus in particular on research published since that date to get a more complete and current picture of the status of the field and locate other articles that address dimensions of interest to you that were not the focus of the literature review.

A literature review will generally include qualitative, quantitative and mixed-methods research, depending on how previous research that is reported was conducted. The reference list can be very useful for locating articles reporting previous research in the area and helping you to identify the *key researchers* in the field as well as the journals publishing their work. You can then find out whether those researchers have published more recently in the field. An American journal that publishes high-quality reviews of research in different areas of education, and that is well worth following, is the *Review of Educational Research*.

Descriptive statistics are calculated on quantitative data and describe that set of data—for example, using percentages, means (mathematical averages), median and mode (the most frequently occurring score). Descriptive statistics are unable to be used to predict how other cohorts might perform in similar situations, as is the case with inferential statistics.

Meta-analyses are similar to literature reviews in that they draw together and critique published research in a particular area. A key difference is that they focus entirely on reports of certain types of quantitative research only, and do not include qualitative research. Not all quantitative research reports are suitable for inclusion in meta-analyses. Studies that report **descriptive statistics** only (often small-scale, quantitative studies) cannot be included. Larger-scale studies that report **effect sizes**, or from which effect sizes can be calculated, are needed. Meta-analyses are able to bring together the findings from many quantitative research reports within an area, leading to conclusions that take account of the collective findings of a large number of quantitative studies rather than focus on the contributions of individual studies only.

Effect size Reports the extent to which the variable of interest accounts for differences in achievement in students who are exposed to that method, compared with students who are not exposed to that method. By implication, the difference that is not found to be attributable to the variable of interest must be attributable to other variables.

If a meta-analysis is found in your area of interest and subject to the parameters of your assignment or the work that you do in your subject or course, you are likely to include it in your literature review. You can also locate and read any of the articles that are included in the meta-analysis.

Other avenues for reporting research include conference presentations and particularly published papers arising from conference presentations. Professional associations that organise conferences may invite presenters to submit written papers based on their presentations and subsequently publish papers that were submitted, and that have been reviewed and accepted for publication. There are often two lists of papers, peer-reviewed and non-peer-reviewed, and these are usually shown as two separate groups on the relevant websites. Peer-reviewed papers that make it through to publication often do so based on favourable evaluations from reviewers whose identities are not revealed to the researchers. This is referred to as *blind peer review*, and is also often used for reviewing articles submitted to journals. In general, it is preferable to

Edited books Different from authored books because the editor or editors are not the authors of all of the chapters. They may write one or more chapters but most chapters will be written by other researchers who may be known for their expertise. It is important to make the distinction between edited and authored books in lists of references or when researchers list their publications.

include relevant peer-reviewed rather than non-peer-reviewed articles in a literature review.

Another avenue for researchers to publish from their work is in **edited books**, in which one or more editors invite chapters on the theme of the book and lead the process through to publication for those chapters that are accepted. Chapters go through a review process that may or may not be blind.

Some researchers also write entire books based on their research. If you find a research-based authored book that is relevant, you may refer to it in your review—particularly if the book is a seminal one in your field. For example, if you see such a book referred to by the authors of evidence-based research articles in your area, you might consider whether this book (or something in it) is important when reviewing the literature in your area.

Book chapters and articles are often written in different ways. Book chapters do not always focus on one specific study, although they may draw on research to develop and present arguments. Another important difference is that books often take longer to reach publication, although certain journals also typically take longer than others. Journals that note the dates of submission and final acceptance on the first pages of the articles that they publish can give you an idea of the range. An article appearing in 2018, for example, may have submission and acceptance dates in 2018 or earlier. It is important, therefore, to turn to journal articles for more recent and current reports of research.

Other types of publications that are sometimes used in literature reviews include *policy documents* produced by education departments or other organisations. Policies should really be informed by research findings in the area, especially if practice is intended to be evidence-based. Policy documents are not written with the purpose of reporting the findings of a particular study. Unless you have a specific reason for doing so, and your lecturer or research supervisor agrees to the inclusion of other documents such as policy documents, you are likely to focus on the other types of publications. Sometimes theses that report research at the Masters or Doctoral levels (and which can be used in literature reviews if appropriate) will need to refer to relevant policy documents—for example, if the research explores or investigates how, or the extent to which, policy priorities or requirements are evident in practice. Often, however, reference to such documents will occur in another part of the thesis, rather than the literature review chapter. For shorter research reports or articles, it is often the case that, because fewer references are usually included, evidence-based research articles and perhaps a limited number of books, book chapters or refereed papers written following conference presentations will be preferred if they report research conducted in the area. The final decision often rests on what you decided, from your wider reading, to use in your literature review.

You may find that most of the research reports that you include in your literature review are evidence-based research articles, particularly those published in peer-reviewed journals. It is important, however, to be aware of any parameters set by your studies. Completing the following exercise in your notebook will help you to establish those parameters.

For your notebook

Exercise 4.1 What types of references are required by your subject or course for your literature review?

Before starting to look for references for your literature review, check your subject or course materials and/or with your lecturer or research supervisor to find out whether there are any particular requirements with regard to the type or number of references that you should be seeking.

For example, if you are not required to undertake a full literature review, but instead to select a small number of recent, evidence-based research articles just to start learning the process, then there may be limitations on the required number and type of references that you are expected to find.

Knowing the parameters before you start your search could save you valuable time and effort.

Label your response 'Exercise 4.1 What types of references are required by your subject or course for your literature review?'

Getting started with your search for references

Important early considerations when commencing work on your literature review include how to recognise evidence-based research articles, where you will find these articles and how you will access them. As noted in Chapter 2, an evidence-based research article typically includes a title, abstract (which may or may not have a heading), literature review, methods section, results and/or findings section/s, discussion and conclusions for future research and perhaps for practice, and a list of references referred to in the article.

The best place to start to look for evidence-based research articles is your university library. University librarians typically provide information and assistance on how to identify and use databases relevant to your discipline so that you can find and locate evidence-based research articles and other relevant research reports in your area of interest. You should inquire early about the information and assistance that is available and whether the library provides training, either more generically or in your discipline. In some situations, you will find very specific online training available as a result of collaboration between the library and academic staff members. Remember, however, that it is your job to learn how the process works and to locate articles; it is not a case of providing a list of your requirements for library staff to do the work for you and find what you need.

The reason why it can be advantageous to go through your university library to access publications that you identify is because university libraries often pay for access to a large number of online journals and other publications to which you may not otherwise have access. In particular, some journals have an embargo period—for example, up to eighteen months from the date of publication of journal issues— and only individuals or organisations with subscriptions to those journals can gain access to the more recent articles. If you locate online journals that do not have open access and without going through your university library, you may not be able to access articles from those journals—or at least more recent articles.

An important point to note is that finding references does not mean just locating references that support your point of view and ignoring those with findings that are different from what you might hope or expect. You should read more broadly and be true to your goal of finding out what is known in your area of interest, putting your opinions to one side. Later you will examine those references to find out how the research was conducted and how key variables were defined, as these details may help to explain why the findings were different and help you achieve a critical, as opposed to descriptive, level of analysis in your literature review.

Another avenue to search for evidence-based research articles that you are advised to use to complement your searches of university library databases is *Google Scholar*. You may still need to be logged into your university to gain access to these articles, but Google Scholar searches are often very effective. When you know of articles that are within your area but you cannot find more recent articles on the same topic, there are ways of identifying such articles. While logged into Google Scholar, you simply click on 'cite' underneath the bibliographic details link to an article to find a list of publications that cited that article. The filter option in the menu on the left can be used to search for any citations that occurred within the current year before systematically adding previous years. You will need to use the links to locate those publications and to see whether they are suitable. I have used this technique many times and highly recommend it.

Annotated bibliography A list of references presented just like a reference list, with a summary paragraph outlining each item under its entry.

As you locate potential literature for your review, it is helpful to construct an **annotated bibliography** by doing a paragraph summary of the main points—similar to an abstract—for each article or other piece of literature. An annotated bibliography is a good starting point for reading more in depth and taking detailed notes of your selected articles, as explained in the next section. It also helps you begin constructing your reference list. The list is presented alphabetically and, as you would do for your reference list, with full bibliographic details.

Once you know who has published in your area of interest, another option is to check whether these researchers have Google Scholar profiles, which list most of their publications. You can sort the publications by year and check for relevance, as well as for more recent articles that cite these researchers' works. It is also worth asking your university librarian about other possible options for locating researcher profiles.

In summary, it is wise to have a number of ways of identifying references in your area. It is also wise to keep a list of the *keywords* or *search terms* that you use when looking for references so that you can be systematic in your approach. If you are not successful with some search terms, try using the same search terms on another day before you dismiss them and replace them with others because sometimes you can be lucky the second time. The reason may be that something new is added to the database or you do something different without realising it when searching again. If you have difficulty locating relevant publications, ask your university librarian for help. Your list of keywords and also your notes about your topic, broad research question, purpose of your research and draft specific research questions can save time because you can show the librarian what you are looking for and what you have already tried.

The following exercise gives you the space to follow through with your own university library to find out what training and resources are available and then to undertake the training. Often, the best training enables you to learn the process of finding reports of evidence-based research in your particular area at the same time as learning generic search skills. Even if you undertook this training within the past year, it is well worth refreshing your skills because the ways in which searches are done can change and the resources available are usually updated frequently.

 For your notebook

Exercise 4.2 What training and resources are available through your university library?

Look at your university library homepage to locate links to training and resources for learning how to search the databases. You will identify keywords or search terms and keep a list of any that you use, together with a list of the databases that you search.

Contact a library staff member who can help you to start searching the databases for evidence-based research articles and other research reports that are relevant to your subject or course requirements.

Then use your keywords to search Google Scholar and follow the ideas from the earlier discussion about this approach. You may still need to experiment with keywords to find appropriate results.

If your searches do not yield results after looking for several days, contact your university librarian again for more help to get started. Ensure that you share with the librarian the keywords, search terms and databases that you have already tried, as well as your brief notes about your topic, broad research question, the purpose of your research and your draft specific research questions.

Your lecturer or research supervisor might also be able to suggest one or more key authors in your area of interest or provide further advice.

The library staff may also know of other resources that you can use that were not initially evident from the library homepage. These could include an introduction to EndNote or other systems that enable you to organise and present your references. While whether to use EndNote is usually an individual decision, many students find that it saves them a lot of time once they are competent with the program. EndNote or other systems, however, do not replace the need to learn about the referencing system (for example, APA) that your lecturer may require you to use.

READING AND TAKING NOTES

Purposefully reading and taking notes on your selected literature is an important step in proceeding towards being able to write your literature review. This step should not be thought of as the writing of the literature review, but the first writing that you do that eventually leads in that direction.

Evidence-based research articles are often very difficult to read until you know a lot more about the research process and you have had considerable experience reading articles. For example, if you do not have a statistical background and you are reading reports of quantitative research, the statistical tables and the text around them may not mean a great deal to you. You should not let this deter you. Often the best way to start is to read the titles and abstracts to do an initial scan of articles in order to decide which ones are relevant and to have a summary of key points. Well-written abstracts and your annotated bibliography will usually lead you to decide whether to put articles in the 'to read' pile (for possible inclusion in your literature review) or to reject them as unsuitable for your purpose. Looking again at the articles in the 'to read' pile will enable you to prioritise which articles will be read first.

It is also worth remembering that evidence-based research articles include a literature review section (which may have a different heading but can be found before the methods section). Paying particular attention to how these literature reviews are structured and written could be very helpful to you later when you develop a structure for, and write, your literature review. Just bear in mind that, while their overall aims may be similar, the literature reviews that you read will show some variation because they are not all on exactly the same topic. It is also important to remember the parameters that you need to follow, which will depend on your course or subject requirements. Even so, it is worth returning to literature reviews in evidence-based research articles several times, reading for different purposes. You will see different ways of developing arguments, ways in which the authors interpret and convey what is known, how previous research was conducted and how they incorporate references into the text.

Before taking notes on your selected articles, there are a few practical points that you may find helpful.

- *Take notes in your own words.* If you copy verbatim from the text, it can be difficult to use your own words later. Writing notes using the other authors' words reinforces those words so much that it can be hard to think of your own words later. It is important not to rely too heavily on direct quotes, even if you ensure that you follow conventions for presenting quotes.
- *Write or print your notes on one side of the paper only.* This is so that you can later view your notes from multiple articles at the same time and highlight points of comparison and difference across the articles. This makes it easier when looking for common or recurring

themes across articles, which is necessary for building your theoretical or conceptual framework and deciding how you will group the articles when writing your literature review.

- *Read the title, abstract and the conclusion of each article to give you an overview before going back to the start to take notes.* The abstract is a summary that provides important information, such as the purpose of the research, the research question/s (these are not always found in the abstract and may appear later), information about the participants, such as the number of participants, the methods of data collection, the main findings from the study and implications for future research and/or practice. The conclusion should be consistent with the abstract, and it is usually there that you will find suggestions for other aspects of the topic not covered by that research and that could or should be the focus of future research. Together with implications for future research, the conclusion will sometimes also point to implications for practice and show how these are drawn from the findings of the study.

The following exercise should be completed with each article.

 For your notebook

Exercise 4.3 Taking notes from evidence-based research articles

Starting with the first article that you prioritised and progressively proceeding to the others, take notes on:

- key information from the *abstract*

- key *themes* discussed in the *introduction and literature review* or theoretical overview, noting the *main authors* whose work is cited or discussed

- whether any *debates* are identified and discussed in the literature review section of the article, and points of agreement or difference made about other researchers' findings. Also note any *definitions of key variables*, as researchers may use different definitions from each other. This is important to know, especially if the findings from studies that appear to be in the same area are different. Including definitions in your notes will be helpful a little later when you make comparisons across articles.

- the research question/s

- key points from the *methods* section of the article, such as details about the *number of participants* and any *characteristics* such as demographics, age range or year levels as appropriate, along with *methods used to select participants* and methods of *data collection and analysis*; and any *limitations* in the research that are identified (or the limitations may be discussed later in the article)

- key *results or findings*

- *implications* for future research or practice

- the *bibliographic details* of each article. Start your reference list using the referencing style required by your course or subject. If you are using the APA (American Psychological Association) referencing system, then your reference list should be labelled simply 'References'.

Note that starting this step now and building your reference list progressively rather than waiting until your literature review is written can save a lot of time and anguish if you later cannot locate easily the bibliographic details that you need.

It is also from these notes that a one-paragraph summary can be produced for an annotated bibliography, which will later facilitate the sorting of the references and how they could be relevant to the review.

Even though you may find other articles that you also wish to add to your list and take notes on later, once you have notes on a selection of articles, you can lay out your notes in front of you on your desk (or you can do the equivalent electronically). Having written or printed your notes on one side of the paper makes it easier to look across the notes for each article and draw out common themes as you work on your conceptual or theoretical framework, which will eventually shape the structure of your literature review.

DELINEATING THEMES AND DEBATES, AND DEVELOPING A CONCEPTUAL FRAMEWORK

As you move from one article to the next, keep going back to your notes from the earlier articles. Look for similarities and differences in themes across the articles. The goal is to draw out the *key themes* and any *debates* that relate to the focus of your study and your research question/s. As you get to know more about the research in your area, your choice of themes will either be confirmed or you will modify your choice as you build your conceptual or theoretical framework to guide the structure of your literature review. Based on your decisions, you may even refine your research questions and later be able to argue how your research questions arise from your critique of the evidence-based research literature in your area of interest, thus addressing the final criterion for developing and refining research questions introduced in Chapter 2.

The process of developing your conceptual framework, therefore begins once you read and take notes on several articles and start to identify themes. You then test your developing framework as you work on each additional article and review your notes from previous articles. This is where being able to place your notes for each article in front of you on your desk is helpful. You can then easily look from one to the other. I find this approach helpful because I will often use different coloured highlighter pens for each theme, so I can see at a glance which articles address the same themes. Later, when writing about each theme, I can easily draw on my notes from the relevant articles. This may mean that some articles are referred to more than once in the literature review, but that is fine because it is expected that you will structure the literature review around the *themes that form your conceptual framework* rather than to proceed from one article or one author to the next.

Throughout this process, there will be times when you need to go back to the articles to check something that you wrote (or did not write) in your notes. You may find that some of the articles you originally thought would be relevant are placed to the side and perhaps not used, or are used more in passing, even if you already took notes from them. As the focus becomes clearer it is likely that you will return to the databases and Google Scholar to check for other articles, perhaps using keywords or search terms that are slightly different from those you used earlier and also the names of authors of articles that you are starting to see as (key) players in the field. This is where having a list of keywords or search terms alongside a list of databases searched previously will be very helpful.

Having a list of the journals where you found your articles can also be useful for going back to those journals and scanning recent issues to see whether there are any other articles that did not emerge through other search methods or newer articles that also need to be considered. As you become engrossed in this work, you may note that the process is an *iterative* one, just like the development of your research question/s. This can be reassuring, particularly if you found that your earlier searches did not yield many results.

Not all authors of evidence-based research articles use the same terms for their themes, and so it is important not to look for keywords only, but also to *read for meaning*. You may even find it necessary to explain how the same ideas are labelled differently or to explain how different researchers used different definitions for the same concepts, even if they used the same labels. If the labels are different, you may even need to decide on what you will call your key themes so that you draw together similar themes under common keywords. Unfortunately, there is no single approach that can be recommended for this part of your work because each literature review is different. You, as the writer, are the conduit between the authors of the collection of evidence-based research articles and the audience for your literature review, and it is your job to find a way to *synthesise what is known* and to *present it authentically* for the first time.

As you read further you may also identify additional themes and you could potentially have quite a few, depending on the articles that you read. It may take quite a lot of thinking to distil just a few themes for your framework and perhaps to see whether some themes are really sub-themes that sit underneath others. You may even need to acknowledge several more themes briefly and to explain how your focus is on just part of the bigger picture, which may not necessarily include these additional themes. The process often involves narrowing the focus in order to define the limits or boundaries of your study and to continue to think small scale. Louise eventually focused on the content and delivery of programs and lifelong learning, Maria focused on engagement and teaching and I focused on pre-service teachers' confidence to solve mathematical problems and confidence to teach mathematical problem solving to others.

Remember that many of the articles you read will be based on larger studies. If you find some studies that not only focus on what interests you but also include other key foci, then you do not necessarily need to include them all, although you may acknowledge the wider scope of some research when identifying the parts that are relevant to your study. Even researchers whose studies are larger in scale will often narrow their focus for individual articles, focusing on one aspect of their research, because articles are much shorter than Doctoral and Masters theses, for example, which are written in chapters. It is difficult to reach depth within a single article if the scope is too wide.

My early reading of articles about self-efficacy revealed that the key figure in the field was Albert Bandura and that the literature reviews of reports of research into self-efficacy drew upon a common set of literature by Bandura. This led me to read his book, *Social Foundations of Thought and Action*, and his articles to help me to understand the concept of self-efficacy, its core components, how it was defined and Bandura's essential principles for designing and conducting research in the area. It provided me with points of comparison when reading and critiquing other research reports into self-efficacy. At another level down, my reading of articles by other authors also led me to identify key researchers who applied Bandura's concept of self-efficacy to my particular area of interest. My conceptual framework therefore drew upon Bandura's definition of self-efficacy and his principles for designing and conducting research into self-efficacy more generally first, referring to his seminal book and articles, and then examined key themes that were evident in research into self-efficacy and mathematics more specifically.

In undertaking her literature review, Louise found that theories on motherhood over time demonstrated an important progression in understanding and defining the concept. She found that motherhood was initially viewed as a state that was attained, but later it was realised that the role of mother developed as children grew and reached different life stages. The mother's role changed as mothers needed to gain new skills and respond to new situations. Louise identified the key players in these two theories of motherhood, and was able to explain why the change in emphasis occurred. She then saw theory about becoming a mother as having parallels with lifelong learning theory, so a conceptual or theoretical framework that she used combined these two previously separate areas. After identifying the big picture, therefore, both Louise and I found it easier to drill down to the details of the components of our conceptual frameworks.

Examples of conceptual frameworks are important because there can be quite a range found in literature reviews. This is because each area is different and because researchers are forging new ground as they identify and seek to address gaps in knowledge or build on previous research. Sometimes, as with Louise's research, there is a historical element and/or two previously separate but complementary areas are combined.

The conceptual or theoretical framework that you build then develops into the structure for your literature review. The parts need to fit together logically, and as your framework develops it can be tested with each new article that you read in the area. Perhaps a later researcher identified and explored or investigated another angle that previous research did not identify, and perhaps it is relevant now to add that angle to your framework or to acknowledge it and to explain or confirm why it is not part of your focus.

It is quite common to get a bit 'stuck' in trying to work out what the pieces are in your conceptual framework, and how those pieces fit together—particularly if it becomes evident that different researchers reached different conclusions and you need to try to work out why. This is where it is not only important to acknowledge how key concepts may have been defined differently in different studies and by different authors, but to look at similarities and differences in methods that were used in these studies. Your notes from each article included details about the methods, and it is important to go back to these notes and often to reread the methods sections of the articles. It could be, for example, that two researchers explored the same area but that the ages or cultural backgrounds of their participants were very different. The differences in the findings could be for a range of possible reasons; it is your job to do some detective work.

If your framework feels comfortable and logical, it can seem as if it were always there, even though you only just developed it. Sometimes, however, it is difficult to see how the parts relate and you spend a lot of time scratching your head, thinking and reading and rereading. It is important to understand that the process is *not often straightforward* and that you will likely go through *periods when there is some confusion*.

It can be very helpful listening to other students talk about their conceptual frameworks and how they see the parts fitting together for their literature reviews. Whenever you get the opportunity to listen to other students or see their ideas, even if their literature reviews are in areas different from your own, it is helpful to take those opportunities. You can then see in action how different frameworks develop and you can also contribute to the discussion. Sometimes your comments can be even more helpful if you are not coming from the same direction because your ideas are likely to be more open and not so fixed. Becoming fixated too soon and before considering other options or reading more widely is not always helpful.

The following exercises are intended to help you with the difficult process of proceeding from your note taking through to having a framework around which you shape your literature review. The first exercise, which can be done at your desk, provides you with the option of developing a table and/or a figure or a diagram to sort your themes and ideas into a structure for a conceptual or theoretical framework. You might like to try both ways and see which one works better for you or for your topic. Some people have a preference for tables and some people prefer figures or diagrams to help them to visualise how the different parts fit together. Alternatively, trying both of these techniques could lead you to develop another approach that you find suits you or your topic better.

For your notebook

Exercise 4.4 Turning notes into tables and figures or diagrams

Return to the notes that you took while reading the articles and look at any highlighted parts of your notes. Summarise your notes in a table, similar to the one below, so that you can easily compare key points across the different articles. Use the number of columns relevant to you, but it can be helpful to start with just a few articles, adding others later.

Area	Article 1 (author/year)	Article 2 (author/year)	Article 3 (author/year)
Abstract			
Key themes/main authors			
Definitions/debates			
Research question/s			
Methods			
Results or findings			
Implications			
Comments			

Now see whether you can turn this information into a figure or diagram that draws on your notes about the topic, problem, broad research question, purpose of your study and your draft specific research question/s. The figure could indicate the connections between these areas and the themes shown in the table. Other detail from the table can be added next, perhaps using a different font.

The following exercise is a group one in which you present your ideas for your (developing) framework orally and visually to other students. If several students present to each other, some may be presenting their ideas up to that point and showing where they are 'stuck', while others may be further along with their frameworks.

 For your notebook

Exercise 4.5 What is your conceptual framework? How do the pieces fit together?

You may now be fairly close to having a framework that you can present orally and visually to others to enable them to ask questions and provide feedback and ideas about the logic of your developing conceptual or theoretical framework.

Present an overview of your topic, broad research question, purpose and the latest iterations of your draft research question/s. Then present your table and talk about the studies that you read, providing more detail as well as identifying common themes. If you have a figure or diagram, you should present that as well.

Alternatively, if you are struggling to see how the parts fit together logically, this can be a very effective forum for presenting your current thinking and opening up the discussion about how the parts connect or could connect. You can invite your audience members to experiment with figures that might help you to get closer to a framework that could work for you or at least bring you closer to the framework that you will use to structure and write your literature review. Be sure to take notes.

Set aside time after the presentation to go through ideas that you noted from the discussion and to draw up headings and sub-headings for your literature review that reflect the conceptual or theoretical framework that you established. After reading and taking notes from any further references that you wish to add and including them in your table, you are probably ready to start noting key points (even in dot point form at this stage) that you will address under each heading (and perhaps sub-heading) when writing your literature review.

Note that *you will not use dot points when writing your literature review*. It is important to write in sentences and paragraphs, with each paragraph consisting of more than one sentence and each section in your review having more than one paragraph.

TAKING YOUR REVIEW FROM THE DESCRIPTIVE TO THE CRITICAL LEVEL

I never worry if a student, having decided on the structure of the literature review, then writes at the descriptive level for some or all of the first draft of the review. I would only worry if the final review of literature were not at a critical level. The question is: *What are these levels and how do you get from the descriptive to the critical level?*

The descriptive level basically involves telling the story. The conceptual framework is still there and you might even draw out similarities and differences between the findings of the studies under each theme. The critical level of analysis provides insights into differences in the way that the studies were conducted that may help to account for the differences in findings. It often helps to ask questions about what you have written.

An example in my own research was when I was looking at research into achievement and learning environments. I found that some previous research favoured cooperation and some favoured competition. A closer look revealed that how cooperative learning environments were defined was not consistent across all the studies, and that the variations in the findings could be accounted for at least in part by the differences in definitions. In fact, it can be misleading to reach conclusions based on comparing findings of studies that used different operational definitions for the same variables.

Looking closely at the methods used in the different studies could provide other reasons why you would not necessarily expect the same findings. The participants might be from different age groups, be doing work at different levels or come from different demographic or cultural backgrounds, or the different groups may have been exposed to the same methods for different lengths of time. There can be many possible reasons for the differences. 'However' statements can sometimes be useful when drawing out these differences. Here is a hypothetical example.

> Smith and Jones (2014) found that struggling readers made significant gains in reading fluency when a particular approach was used; however, a similar study conducted by Joyce and Barratt (2014) at around the same time found that struggling readers with similar reading fluency at the outset made very little progress when the same method was used.

You may be unable to be conclusive about the reasons for the different findings, but a closer look at the methods employed in each study could provide some possible insights.

For your notebook

Exercise 4.6 Taking the literature review from the descriptive to the critical level

Once you have a draft of your literature review, you are ready to examine it closely to determine whether your writing is descriptive or whether a critical level of analysis is starting to emerge.

First check that your review conveys not just what is known about your area and is in line with your topic, broad research question, the purpose of your study and your specific research question/s, but that you included information on how the studies to which you referred were conducted.

Ask yourself questions such as the following, revisiting your notes and the original articles if further information needs to be added in your literature review:

- Does the review convey what is known from previous research about your area of interest?

- Is this in line with your topic, broad research question, the purpose of your study and your specific research question/s?

- Did you specifically point to similarities and differences in the findings of the various studies with reference to the areas of relevance to your study?

- Does the review include information about how the studies to which you referred were conducted?

- Is there enough information around the methods to show similarities and differences in the ways that the different studies were conducted, including information around the participants?

- Do you provide suggestions or possible reasons why the findings from different studies might be different?

> • Does your concluding paragraph show how your research fits into or adds another angle or dimension to previous research? These points may be alluded to in relevant places throughout your review.

After working through the next section of the chapter, you will also be able to ensure that your specific research question/s appear towards the end of your literature review.

REFINING YOUR RESEARCH QUESTIONS

Once your literature review is complete, you should be able to refine your research question/s or confirm your draft question/s and argue how your study, as encapsulated in your research question/s, has the potential to advance knowledge in the area. By seeing how your study can fit into what is already known, your research questions can address the final criterion for developing and refining research questions introduced in Chapter 2. Knowing how previous research was conducted and thinking about your context and your position as a novice researcher who needs to fit your research into your course or subject requirements, you might start to see how your research could be conducted and how that might also be reflected in your research questions.

Depending on what you found when completing your literature review, it may be necessary to make further modifications to your specific research question/s, or even to your broad research question, purpose statement or statement of your problem. How you see the big picture fitting together now after having examined previous research in the area could change or it could remain the same—or much the same. For Louise, it meant that her focus on finding out from mothers in her young parents program what they thought about the content and delivery of her program could remain the same, but she might need to be more cognisant of the age and stage of development of their babies. This was because more recent literature recognises that motherhood is not a state that is attained, but a role that constantly develops and changes as babies become toddlers and toddlers grow into early childhood. In fact, it is now recognised that the role of mother changes across the lifespan of the child. What prospective mothers want to know (content of the program), for example, could change once the baby is born, and then later as the baby reaches different milestones in development. Mothers' preferences for how the program is delivered could also depend not only on the stage of development of their own baby, but the age of the babies of the other mothers taking the program at the same time. The findings would then need to relate back to these variables. In summary, while Louise's research questions may have remained fairly similar after she completed her literature review, she was a little wiser about these points and could even have brought the age of babies into her research questions if she wished.

Whenever research questions undergo refinements, it is important to go back to the set of criteria for developing and refining research questions that were introduced in Chapter 2. This is to ensure that any changes—for example, ones that made closer connections between the research questions and the findings from previous research literature—could mean that one or more other criteria are not met as well as they were previously. The concluding exercise guides you through a reassessment of your specific research questions, which are then added to the end of your literature review.

CONCLUDING EXERCISE

 For your notebook

Exercise 4.7 Refining your specific research questions

Revisit the current iteration of your specific research question/s addressing the criteria below. Make changes to your question/s as necessary. If you make any changes to the wording of your specific research question/s, ensure that you work through the criteria again for a final check.

- the *purpose* of your research, your topic, problem and broad research question

- your course *requirements, timeframe, time available and capacity* as a novice researcher

- the *context* in which your research will be conducted

- the *participants* or participant groups of interest

- the person or persons *to whom your research would matter* and how it would *inform your practice*

- the *type of data* (qualitative, quantitative or mixed methods) needed to be collected

- the need for the research questions to be *simple, not too long, clear and easily understood*

- possible *ethical issues or dilemmas*

- *how well the specific research questions connect with each other* (if you have more than one)

- *previous research* (as reported in evidence-based research articles and from your literature review).

CHAPTER SUMMARY

In this chapter, you took the time to:

- identify and locate relevant literature for possible inclusion in your literature review, using keywords from your topic and problem

- read widely in your area of interest and narrow the focus before deciding on which evidence-based research articles and other literature you would include in your literature review

- read purposefully and take notes on your selected articles and other literature

- draw out themes and debates, and construct a conceptual or theoretical framework for your literature review

- decide on the structure of your literature review, draft your review and engage with techniques to take your review of the literature from the descriptive to the critical level

- review and refine your specific research questions using the framework introduced in Chapter 2

- read definitions of important key terms: annotated bibliography, conceptual or theoretical framework, descriptive statistics, edited books, effect size, literature review, meta-analysis, research design.

FURTHER READING

Gay, L.R., Mills, G.E. & Airasian, P.W. (2012), *Educational Research: Competencies for analysis and applications* (10th ed.), Upper Saddle River, NJ: Pearson Education. See pp. 79–100.

McMillan, J.H. & Schumacher, S. (2010), *Research in Education: Evidence-based inquiry* (7th ed.), Upper Saddle River, NJ: Pearson Education.
See pp. 26–44, 72, and particularly pp. 77 and 93–6.
Pyrczak, F. (2017), *Evaluating Research in Academic Journals: A practical guide to realistic evaluation* (6th ed.), Glendale, CA: Pyrczak Publishing.
See Chapter 4 and Chapter 5.

5
Understanding research designs

This chapter will help you to:

 consider a range of research designs, including their key features and how different designs are appropriate for different research questions

 select a research design to address your research question/s and justify your choice.

Planning your research involves making many decisions. This is evident at each stage of the planning. It begins with deciding on a topic and which part of the topic or particular problem you will pursue, then moves to deciding how to articulate the broad research question, the purpose of the research and the specific research question/s. Many of these decisions are influenced by what interests, excites or challenges you, or makes you curious, the *context* in which you would like to conduct your research and the findings of *previous research* in the area.

Once you make these decisions, the next steps involve determining your broad framework or *research design* and your *methods of data collection* and *data analysis*, all of which need to relate to your research question/s. The clarity of focus and the consistency and internal logic that you worked so hard to achieve when developing your early ideas need to continue as you plan the next stages of your small-scale research project.

It is important to take a philosophical approach to deciding on your research design. This is because choosing a research design not only involves arguing why one design is appropriate and fit for purpose, but why other designs are less appropriate or even inappropriate. As your ideas begin to develop, they will be tested as you learn about other research designs. You may reject some designs quite early because your research question clearly points to the collection of either qualitative or quantitative data, and your research design needs to accommodate that focus. You are strongly encouraged to begin by thinking of each design as a plausible contender before you reject it or place it aside for further consideration. Novice researchers planning small-scale studies need to understand the key features of the main research designs and even more about their chosen research design and close contenders.

The requirements of your course or subject will determine how deeply and to what extent you need to explain why you chose one design and not others. Your writing will reflect your breadth and depth of understanding (or misunderstanding), even in a passage in which you explain your chosen design before justifying your choice. Experienced researchers will know from your use of language and how you articulate your ideas whether you really understand the basic differences between your chosen design and other designs, or even the differences between qualitative and quantitative approaches.

When considering which design is most suitable for addressing your research question, it is important to continue to think *small scale*. A common problem experienced by novice researchers is that their research questions are more appropriate for larger-scale studies. If your ideas have several parts or point to a *longitudinal study*, then it can be helpful to consider focusing on just one part, so your small-scale study is one phase of something that could be bigger. Either you or another researcher could pick up and continue with the other phases later. There is still time now to refine your specific research question/s to achieve the scale that you need as you consider the appropriateness of each design.

Even when research questions are suitable for small-scale studies and appear to be sound and considerable learning and thinking about research designs has begun, finding a suitable research design can sometimes seem elusive. If the match is hard to achieve then the *problem is often with the research question*, which should reflect what you wish to discover. Researchers frequently toggle back and forth between their research questions and their ideas around research design. This is not a problem: it is just another part of the *iterative process* of developing suitable research questions and ensuring consistency and an internal logic between all parts of the research plan. It only becomes a problem if the mismatch between the research questions and the research design persists into the next stages of planning and conducting the study.

The first section of this chapter introduces a challenging, hypothetical classroom scenario or problem before asking you to brainstorm a range of research questions that could fit the scenario. The following sections of the chapter then describe the key features, uses and limitations of qualitative, quantitative and mixed-methods research designs, respectively. These sections of the chapter provide the opportunity for you to consider the *suitability of the research designs for different research questions*, including research questions related to the classroom scenario and your own topic, problem, broad research question and purpose statement.

In addition to deciding which design will address your research question/s, you can also begin to discern *why other designs may not be appropriate*. Further suggested reading about your chosen design in particular is advised once you work through the reading and exercises in this chapter. You can then interrogate your chosen research design and other aspects of it more deeply. The chapter concludes with suggestions for further reading, from which you can select readings that are most appropriate to you.

HYPOTHETICAL CLASSROOM SCENARIO OR PROBLEM FOR INVESTIGATION

The teacher in this scenario observed that many students in the class did not produce very much writing during creative writing lessons and that the hardest part appeared to be getting the students started with their writing. Most of the lesson time was allocated to writing, so it seemed as if the amount of time available for writing was not really the problem.

The teacher then recalled a conversation with another teacher over lunch. The other teacher mentioned a YouTube clip on a website that showed a teacher in the United Kingdom some years ago using a computer game called *Myst* to motivate his middle primary class to think creatively and to talk with considerable excitement about their ideas before they started writing. The students were highly enthusiastic and demonstrated noticeable improvements in their ability to articulate their ideas and in a number of areas of writing, which was reflected in their increased literacy scores. The teacher, Tim Rylands, received a BECTA award for his excellent teaching.

After further thinking, talking with colleagues and reading, the teacher whose students needed to do more writing during their creative writing lessons started to theorise that perhaps something different needed to occur at the start of the creative writing lessons to help the students formulate ideas that appealed to them and that they were motivated to pursue in their creative writing. The teacher then brainstormed the following questions:

- How do other teachers in the school teach creative writing?
- What methods do exemplary teachers use to teach creative writing?
- What reasons do teachers give for the ways they teach creative writing?
- Do all teachers in the school find it difficult to motivate children to write during creative writing lessons?
- How much writing do children in other classes produce during their creative writing lessons?
- Why do some of the students in the class produce more writing than others?
- Do children who enjoy their creative writing lessons write more than children who derive less enjoyment from their lessons?

The following exercise for your notebook asks you to think about the scenario and what you would like to find out if you were the teacher or you were intending to conduct research in this area. Your ideas may be similar to or different from the teacher's theory. Of course, if you were intending to plan research in this area, you would also complete a literature review, which would impact on your decisions and may change the particular questions that you develop for this hypothetical exercise. You may even start to think that perhaps the amount students write during their creative writing lessons is not the central concern. Perhaps the quality of writing is more important. Perhaps the discussion over lunch introduced in the scenario above also shifted your thinking.

 For your notebook

Exercise 5.1 What would you be curious to know?

Read the creative writing scenario again and brainstorm a number of other questions that could be starting points for research ideas in this area.

The scenario or description of the problem deliberately does not include a lot of detail. This is so that you can think of a broad range of questions that make you curious and you can add your own details—for example, around year level.

Include some questions that imply the collection or generation of qualitative data and some that imply quantitative data to help broaden your thinking. (Note, for example, that Question 1 in the scenario relates to qualification and Question 7 relates to quantification.)

Add your list of questions to those suggested above and keep the full list of questions for later exercises and as you begin to learn about qualitative, quantitative and mixed-methods research designs.

Label your response 'Exercise 5.1 What would you be curious to know?'

QUALITATIVE RESEARCH DESIGNS: KEY FEATURES, USES AND LIMITATIONS

The first feature about qualitative research that is often mentioned is that the *data are in the form of words rather than numbers*. Researchers are more interested in what people say or what they write, for example, than their scores on tests or other data that are in the form of measurements.

Perhaps a less obvious feature of qualitative research designs is that they are *not concerned with testing theories*, such as in quantitative research that might be concerned with the extent to which one method of teaching creative writing is more effective than another method or whether there is a positive correlation between students' levels of enjoyment of creative writing and how many words they write in class. Instead, *qualitative research designs* focus more on exploring or developing an understanding of how people perceive situations or events, for example. In fact, research questions guiding qualitative research may be less specific because researchers are likely to place a greater premium on hearing participants' stories or their versions or accounts, and allowing themes to emerge from those accounts. Thus qualitative research is concerned with building theory or contributing to our understanding of existing theory in a particular area through exploration rather than through testing.

For example, the research question could focus on exploring what teachers believe to be key reasons for the amount of writing or the quality of writing that students produce in creative writing lessons. Reasons should then emerge in the responses that teachers provide. It may transpire that teachers talk about many other factors that they believe impact on student writing and do not mention enjoyment. If conducting interviews with teachers to explore these ideas, researchers need to be very good at asking questions that encourage teachers to talk, and they also need to be good listeners. They will often ask a small number of open-ended questions that do not reflect their own personal preferences or biases but are open to teachers' own ideas. This point will be pursued further in Chapter 6, which focuses on research methods.

There are a number of qualitative research designs, just as there are quantitative research designs. Some designs are more suitable for novice researchers who have limited timeframes and experience, although that does not imply that some types of qualitative research are relatively easy: they are all complex. The trick is to think small scale and to be realistic about all aspects of the planning, while also being very clear about the purpose of the research. Involving a smaller number of participants and using one or two methods of data collection or data generation can help to ensure that the problem is explored in some depth and the workload is manageable.

Here we will look at a few qualitative designs. You can think about which designs could be more feasible for you if you follow the suggestions above around being mindful of the scale of your study and being realistic and clear in terms of what you can achieve, matching this with the purpose of your study. If you involve one or just a few participants and provide convincing arguments about why it is important for you to have such a small sample, referring back to the purpose of your research and how you anticipate the findings to be useful, you will go a long way towards countering criticisms of your approach. Later you can do further reading on qualitative research designs and also look at others if appropriate. Our main focus will be on introducing case studies, ethnographies, narrative research and action research.

Case studies

Case studies are worth talking about first because it is possible to draw parallels with the scenario about creative writing and because I think that they will resonate with other topics that might be of particular interest to you. If you are interested in following Louise's research on her program for young parents or Maria's research on preparing pre-service teachers to engage with and teach Aboriginal students, you can look at published reports of their research and the types of case studies they conducted. Without this being her original intention, one strand of Maria's later research turned into a longitudinal study of the group of pre-service teachers who were her sample in her early research. While case studies may include both qualitative and quantitative data, they are discussed here because they are often qualitative only and, particularly when that happens, they can be suited to small-scale research. Some researchers even regard all qualitative research as case studies.

Previously, we talked about research problems and how to develop research ideas around problems. One of the draft research questions brainstormed at the end of our scenario early in this chapter was 'What methods do exemplary teachers use to teach creative writing?'

The thinking behind this question was that just because we identify a problem, this does not mean that we necessarily need to focus on situations or cases where teaching is not going to plan. In fact, the idea that something else needs to happen at the beginning of the creative writing lesson to get students motivated and able to write more easily could be an assumption that will not necessarily lead to an answer to the problem. We could do a literature review to see whether there are other clues, but for the moment we could imagine that the problem is a bit of a mystery so we will now think differently about it. It seems already that a qualitative approach may be justified because *we do not really have a theory to test* and *the answer may be found in one or more of a number of different directions*. Depending on the outcomes of a literature review in which we find out what is known about the area, perhaps our research could help to *build theory* or *contribute to existing theory* about the problem. The problem was presented very simply at first: as students not writing enough during creative writing lessons. Perhaps this is just the starting point—the one that most obviously needed a solution.

One suggestion is to turn the research around. Instead of looking at a situation in which something has gone wrong, we could look at a **case** or a few cases of what might be regarded as exemplary practice. If we can find out what is going 'right' or what appears to be going well and explore the case or cases deeply, we may get some ideas that could be tried in other situations where we would like to see similar outcomes.

Case A complete entity that is distinctive in its own right. A small-scale study is likely to focus on a case that is close to home, such as a teacher, a school, a program or a class rather than an educational or cultural organisation, an institution or a nation. Cases are also described by type, such as different types of single case studies or a multiple case study.

One approach a case study could take is to explore how one or more teachers who are considered to be highly effective teachers of creative writing approach their teaching of the subject. Previous research in education examined the characteristics of effective teachers, but this research could focus on the teaching of creative writing. In order to allow for in-depth exploration of exemplary teaching, you could decide that one case would be well worthwhile and sufficient for your purpose. How you identify the case might be another story, but you could imagine observing the teacher in action on at least several occasions, listening to the teacher's account of what he or she does and why, looking at documentation that the teacher might show and discuss, perhaps even observing students and the interaction between the teacher and the students and student-to-student interaction during lessons, as well as talking with students, looking at samples of work and inviting students and teacher to talk about the samples and the teaching behind them. You could aim to draw out the complexity of the case in the words of the participants in the study. One case could potentially involve a number of participants and approaches to data collection.

This research could be an ideal case to which to apply Punch and Oancea's (2014) suggestion that, based on your findings, you might put forward one or more *propositions*—or, to use a term more common in quantitative research, hypotheses—for how to teach creative writing effectively. In fact, your interest might not just be in effective teaching, but in exemplary teaching and how exemplary practice is developed, which again points to the type of case study you might conduct.

There are different types of case studies, and they are described variously in the research methods literature. An approach such as the one we are discussing here involves choosing a case because it is one that you want to explore deeply and you want to understand, so you learn what motivates this exemplary teacher. This goes back to your curiosity about finding out what you want to know. Punch and Oancea (2014) might describe this case as *intrinsic* because your curiosity is piqued by this particular case and what makes it special.

Some researchers start with a single case such as this one, then later add another case and then a few more. How many cases they eventually examine may depend on the point at which they discover that what they learned by examining the earlier cases is being reflected in what they continue to learn in later cases and that new ideas are no longer forthcoming—or what is referred to as *saturation point*. By looking at each case on its own and then making comparisons between the cases and the *themes* that emerge around how exemplary teachers teach creative writing, the evidence starts to accumulate. The emphasis here is clearly on **theory building** or contributing to existing theory, rather than **theory testing**. To put it another way that is common in the literature, the emphasis is on words and working through **inductive analysis** (qualitative) rather than **deductive analysis** (quantitative). Researchers who come in at the point at which theory is already developing (perhaps because of their close examination of one or more intrinsic cases) might be more interested in what Punch and Oancea (2014) and others describe as an **instrumental case study**, which aims to sharpen a developing theory.

The other type of case study identified by a number of authors is a **multiple case study**. The researcher sets out with the intention of examining several cases simultaneously. This approach enables researchers to *draw comparisons and look for points of difference* that together help them to explore the phenomenon of interest.

Even though Bryman (2016) and others recognise that multiple case

Theory building Involves working inductively and drawing out themes from the data that become the building blocks for theory development. It is commonly associated with qualitative research.

Theory testing means beginning with a theory that is proposed at the outset and then using quantitative data to test the theory.

Inductive analysis The way the researcher moves from the data collection through to the identification and discussion of the themes or patterns that emerge from the analysis of the data. Researchers use different strategies depending on their particular study and how they operate, but there should be a clear, underlying logic in the process.

Deductive analysis Begins with a theory and collecting data to test the theory. Working deductively to test theory is usually associated with quantitative research.

Instrumental case study A case study that aims to sharpen a developing theory.

Multiple case study Where the researcher sets out with the intention of examining several cases simultaneously.

studies are quite common now, you should not feel obliged to take on more than one case just because you think that your study would not be good enough if it is restricted to a single case. Thinking about the type of case and fit for your purpose, an intrinsic, single case study as described here could be well argued. The main consideration might be where you make your cut-off in terms of how many methods of data collection you use or how many participants you involve, and the extent to which they are involved.

It often helps to think more extensively at first, as we did above when thinking about observations, interviews, documents, the teacher and students, and then pare back to what is reasonable for you but gives you enough scope. It is a similar process to that used in Chapter 1 to identify more broadly a number of topics that made you curious, from which you later decided on the topic that you would follow. This process will be continued in Chapter 6, where you look more closely at the methods that you will use in your research. In a similar way, learning about *ethnographic research*, *narrative research* and *action research*, and looking at each as a serious contender for your topic, problem and research question, will help you to decide on a qualitative research design that may be appropriate to you, and for which you can present convincing arguments.

Ethnographic research

Knowing a little about case study research provides a head start to beginning to learn about ethnographic research. In fact, Creswell (2012) describes a case study as a form of **ethnography**. He also points out how ethnographers study long-standing groups that share a common culture and how ethnographers immerse themselves in the field over a period of

> **Ethnography** The study of groups over a period of time through immersion in the field and a variety of research methods for the collection of data.

time to understand the group. Ethnography uses a variety of methods such as observing behaviours, listening to what members of the group say during interviews and studying artefacts, such as documents, from the field.

Returning to the idea of a case study on an exemplary teacher of creative writing, an ethnographer might be interested in studying the group of teachers in the faculty where the creative writing teacher works—especially if there is a particular culture present, such as a pursuit for excellence in teaching and learning that distinguishes the faculty or sets it apart. Considerable time would be spent examining what teachers do in their day-to-day practice, examining documents and talking with or interviewing the teachers and others to develop an understanding of the culture of the group.

In the case of the writing scenario, this emphasises how assumptions about the number of words that students write (or do not write) during their creative writing lessons may not be the key or the only point of concern, but that in observing the teachers over time and listening to their accounts while putting our own thoughts to one side opens the way to develop a deeper understanding of the practice of teaching creative writing. It is during this extended period of exploration that ethnographers will likely develop further research questions and even adjust their methods of investigation in their endeavours to understand the culture of excellence in the faculty where creative writing is taught.

We can see here how the way in which research designs are categorised—in this case, related to qualitative research—can blur. As you read research methods literature more broadly, you will appreciate why different authors present information around research designs in different ways. This can be quite confusing, especially for the novice researcher. My suggestion is to keep your research simple and remember the parameters of your course or subject. You do not need to learn everything when conducting your first, small-scale study, but you will be surprised at how much you learn even then!

While you might be less inclined to employ an ethnographic design for your small-scale research because of the timeframe involved and the amount of data that would need to be organised and analysed, having some understanding of ethnography could be helpful for reflecting on your chosen design, its strengths and limitations. These are important considerations for developing arguments regarding the suitability of your chosen design and why other designs were not chosen.

Narrative research

We return here to our classroom scenario and the problem with motivating students to write during their creative writing lessons and the draft research question, 'What methods do exemplary teachers use to teach creative writing?'

As our ideas develop around the scenario and the thought that we could turn our curiosity to how exemplary teachers teach creative writing, it also occurred to me that an individual exemplary teacher may have a story to tell that could enlighten us not only about how the teacher teaches but how he or she got to the point of being regarded as exemplary. The story may reveal, for example, that the teacher previously experienced the same or similar difficulties as the teacher in the scenario, but I would be curious to know what events occurred or how the now-exemplary teacher turned the situation around. We can postulate as to the combination of events that may have occurred, the trigger points, perhaps some mentoring, perhaps a critical incident or a turning point followed by experimentation and deep reflection, but we will only really know by *listening to the teacher's story* or chronological account of events—perhaps over his or her entire teaching career. The story could be immensely informative on a number of levels: it could act as a catalyst for change in other teachers; it could influence professional development activities; and it could provide a sense of optimism or encouragement for other teachers. The exemplary teacher might also feel encouraged.

The idea of asking the teacher to tell the story could encapsulate the main steps in setting up and conducting a *narrative research design* drawn together by Creswell (2012) and highlighted above, including *identifying an individual teacher* whose experiences are of real interest to us and *providing the teacher with the opportunity to relate those teaching experiences as a story*. The initial thinking and planning would be reflected in the choice of topic, the description of the problem, the broad research question, the purpose of the research and statements around why the idea is important and to whom, as well as who might benefit from this research.

A narrative research design could potentially suit our problem scenario, and you may even see that it is a contender for your research. As Bell (2010) points out, narrative inquiry, like the other designs, can have its challenges—particularly for novice researchers working within limited timeframes—but it could still be within reach. Further reading, thinking and discussion would be necessary to build a strong case for adopting or rejecting this research design. Looking carefully at different designs at this early stage opens up other possibilities, just as we have done with our scenario. Again, this is why the iterative process of toggling back and forth between your earlier planning—for example, around the topic, problem, research questions and accompanying statements—to learning about different research designs and selecting a suitable design is important.

Action research

If you were to think of conducting **action research** into the problem of how to increase students' writing outputs during creative writing lessons, you would need to make your own practice your main focus rather than the practices of one or more other teachers. A recurring theme and point of agreement among writers of research methods literature is that action research involves *systematically examining one's own practice*, using a *cycle of planning, acting, observing and reflecting* that is similar to the teaching cycle with which educators are familiar. The emphasis on being systematic is important because it is the idea of being deliberately systematic that sets research apart from everyday practice and, in the case of action research, bringing together the distinctive but complementary areas of action *and* research. A question that you could ask yourself after completing research in action is how the systematic study of the problem changed your approach to teaching or changed the outcomes for your students.

Action research A process of systematically examining one's own practice, using a cycle of planning, acting, observing and reflecting.

Maria could have conceived of her research as action research, but to do so she would need to bring the four parts of the cycle into her planning (possibly repeating them), her conduct of the research and her reporting of the findings. She would need to read the work of key players in the field of action research, such as Kemmis and McTaggart (1988) and others, who draw the distinction between action research and everyday practice. She would also consider who would be her *collaborators* in this action research project. Given that her research responded to the concerns expressed by pre-service teachers regarding their ability to teach Aboriginal students during their practice teaching and later as practising teachers, and her collaboration with a local Elder and Aboriginal community, she would have starting points for considering with whom she might work. She might consider adding to her design an opportunity each week to *reflect* with the pre-service teachers and the Elder on the lessons and *actions* implemented in the community that week and together *plan* what needs to happen next week. The program that she implemented was planned *specifically for her context*, but in reflecting at the end she and her collaborators may have been able to consider how the outcomes of the research could impact more broadly at her university or even further afield.

Action research is like a repeating cycle that spirals outwards and upwards, starting with a specific problem in a specific context but having the potential to affect practice more widely. If you adopt this design, however, you should take care to keep your ideas *small-scale*, confining your approach to working with a *small number of people*, being particularly aware of your *timeframe* and *not collecting or generating too much data*. In retrospect, Maria was probably wise not to use action research for her study. Her timeframe, the number of people involved—including pre-service teachers, Elder and community members, children and parents—and making time to learn about the research design and how it could apply to her research question would have presented practical challenges for her.

The following exercise for your notebook invites you to articulate your initial thoughts around how your own research idea could possibly fit within an action research design and also to consider the challenges that you might face that could potentially preclude you from taking this direction, or that you may need to consider. You may see synergies or differences between your research idea and Maria's research that may help you to identify reasons for and against choosing this design for yourself. These are broad ideas only: you will need to do further reading and thinking if you consider that action research could be a serious contender for you.

 For your notebook

Exercise 5.2 Applying action research to a small-scale study

Write down your current thoughts about the research that you are planning to conduct. Include your:

- topic

- statement of the problem

- broad research question

- purpose statement

- statements about why your research is important and to whom

- one or two specific research questions.

Provide some initial thoughts in dot point form that you might need to consider for each stage of a single cycle:

- plan
- act
- observe
- reflect.

Keep your ideas confined to your particular context.

Next consider and write down the challenges that you anticipate you would face in using an action research design for your small-scale study.

Label your response 'Exercise 5.2 Applying action research to a small-scale study'.

QUANTITATIVE RESEARCH DESIGNS: KEY FEATURES, USES AND LIMITATIONS

When teachers reflect on their practice, they often start to *form theories* for why certain events occur or how those events could be related to each other, make decisions based on their theories and then follow through with actions and observations to *test their theories*. If the theory seems promising, then they may continue with their actions and observations, and reflect on what they find in order to inform their future practice.

A scenario such as the creative writing one is an example of how a classroom problem that needs to be solved could be the catalyst for systematically planning and conducting a type of *experiment* to test a theory that could lead to increasing the amount that students write during creative writing lessons. A teacher who had the opportunity to learn how to approach the problem systematically, and to plan and conduct a study to address the problem, would go through the processes of identifying the *topic and problem*, establish a *broad research question* and a *purpose* for the study and think about *why* research in the area could be important and to whom it might be important. One or more *specific research questions* would be developed and then refined after completing a *literature review* to discover what previous research in the area found and how that research was conducted.

The teacher, now a novice researcher, would then be where you are at present, with the ideas and research questions that you developed in earlier chapters—that is, at the point of determining the most suitable *research design to* frame the approach to the study. Research questions can still undergo further *refinement*, as it is important to continue to *check for and achieve alignment* between the research questions and all other aspects of the research plan.

Broadly, quantitative research designs can be considered in two categories: *experimental* and *non-experimental*. At the centre of both is a theory that the researcher wishes to test through the collection and analysis of *quantitative data* (data in the form of numbers or words that are converted to numbers). This part of the chapter will address experimental designs first, followed by non-experiments.

Experimental research designs

Experimental research designs include *true experiments* (often just called **experiments**) and *quasi-experiments*, but can also cater for experiments involving one or just a few participants, known as *single-subject designs* (McMillan & Schumacher, 2010). All three types of experiments are capable of determining whether one variable, such as a method for teaching creative writing (the *independent variable*) causes a change in another variable (the **dependent variable**, which is measured). For example, a researcher may be interested in determining whether a new method for teaching creative writing (an *intervention* developed to address the problem) leads to *significant* increases in the amount of writing that students produce during lessons compared to the regularly used method.

A true experiment involves *randomly allocating* individual students to either a *control group* or an *experimental group*. The control group is taught creative writing using the old or regular approach, and the experimental group is taught creative writing using the new approach or *intervention*. The amount that students write in each group is measured and compared to find out whether students in one group write significantly more during their creative writing lessons than the students in the other group.

Experiment Experimental and quasi-experimental designs have some features in common but only (true) experiments randomly allocate participants to the control and experimental groups. In schools, the need for classes to remain intact usually means that quasi-experiments are used.

Dependent variables Variables that are measured. For example, achievement in spelling could be measured by administering spelling tests to students working in Method A and Method B so that the methods of teaching spelling (the independent variable) can be compared.

The outcome of the experiment is *hypothesised*, or predicted, before the experiment starts in order to test a theory based on consideration of the findings of previous or related research in the area. Involving (usually) a large number of students and randomly allocating them to the two groups is undertaken so that other variables that could also impact on the *dependent variable* (the amount that students write) such as their ability, are controlled as far as possible by each student having an equal chance of being randomly allocated to either the control or experimental groups.

While a true experiment may appear to be a feasible design for our scenario, it is likely that one requirement could be difficult to meet in a school context, regardless of how many students or classes are involved. It is most unlikely that individual students could be randomly allocated to the control group (the one using the old approach) and the experimental group (the classes using the new approach). This is because of practical issues and possible *ethical concerns* around changing the existing composition of classes for the purpose of conducting the experiment. It is unlikely that a novice researcher would be able to convince the principal (or more than one principal if classes from more than one school were involved), teachers, students and their parents that this should be done.

In this case and others like it, the alternative is to keep the classes intact and *allocate the classes* (rather than individual students) and their teachers to the control and experimental groups. This change would mean that the research design is now a **quasi-experiment** because the classes would remain intact. It is often for practical reasons that quasi-experiments are much more commonplace than true experiments in classroom research.

Quasi-experiment Involves randomly allocating groups such as classes rather than individuals to control and experimental groups. This type of experiment is common in educational settings.

Having decided that a quasi-experiment could be more appropriate than a true experiment for this classroom research, there are many more points for the researcher to consider in the next stage of the planning. For example, it may be wise to obtain *measures of students' performances* on the *dependent variable* (how much students write) before the quasi-experiment starts so that pre-test measures or scores can be taken into account when comparing the performances of the control and experimental groups at the end. In that case, the pre-test scores act like golf handicaps, putting everyone on an even playing field so that the two approaches to teaching creative writing can be compared meaningfully. This is particularly important in quasi-experiments because the students are not randomly allocated to the control or experimental groups, so there is likely to be some variation between the groups on the dependent variable before the experiment begins. *True experiments* may not require pre-testing unless, as indicated by McMillan and Schumacher (2010), the number of participants in each group is less than fifteen. This is a point to investigate further if you consider that a true experiment is appropriate for your research.

Experimental research can also include more than one dependent variable, and sometimes this is appropriate. The more variables involved, however, the more complex the research may become and the scale of your work and how much you need to learn within a short period of time can increase exponentially. As Bell (2010) points out, where there are multiple variables to control, larger sample sizes are needed for a well-designed experiment. As a novice researcher, it is generally advisable not to have too many dependent variables and to keep the research as uncomplicated as possible.

An example of another point to consider is how many lessons would be conducted and the length of time over which the research would occur. In making these decisions, the novice researcher would think about practical issues such as the *timeframe* for completing the study as dictated by requirements of the course or subject and the *number of lessons* that the students might need to take before *differences* in the amount written under each approach would be likely to become apparent. In a small-scale study, there is still the need to allow sufficient time and opportunity for the new method to take effect, but also the need to be practical in terms of your own timelines and the expectations placed on the teachers and students involved in the study.

There are many different ways in which the finer details of quasi-experiments can operate or be conceptualised. One consideration is that not all quasi-experiments have control groups. An experimental group is often thought of as having something that a control group does not have, such as access to additional opportunities or resources or a new method of teaching. In Chapter 3, we discussed practical and ethical issues. Sometimes, however, it is not logical to have a control group because the comparison is not between a group that has something and another group that does not have something, but simply between two currently used approaches that are compared—such as two approaches that teachers use for teaching creative writing. The important point to remember is that the different approaches need to be defined at the outset so that teachers involved in the experiment know the parameters to be followed when using the approach or method allocated to their class. The researcher also needs to demonstrate that the two methods used by the classes operated during the research according to the definitions established at the outset. Such demonstration increases confidence in the findings of the research because it is clear that the approaches being compared were implemented faithfully and strictly.

The third type of experimental research described by McMillan and Schumacher (2010) and McMillan and Wergin (2010), the *single-subject design*, could also be of interest to novice researchers who are interested in comparing the effects of different approaches to teaching creative writing with just one or a few students, have a short timeframe and need their research to be small-scale.

For example, perhaps one particular child or just a few children in the class are the main cause for concern, and there is quite a big difference between the amount of work that this child or these few children produce during their creative writing classes and that produced by the remainder of the children. A single-subject design would enable you to record the number of words that each child writes during the creative writing lessons that use one method and then take the observations again with the same child or children when the other method is used. As suggested by McMillan and Schumacher (2010), the experiment could end at that point or you could repeat the first or both parts. Table 5.1 shows these three possible variations in the single-subject design. The observations are taken during the implementation of each method and comparisons are made across the observations taken with each method for each individual participant or subject in the study. The variation chosen depends on the timeframe for implementing the study and practical classroom considerations, with the most rigorous variation being the third one.

Table 5.1 Variations of the single-subject experimental design

	Time 1	Time 2	Time 3	Time 4
Variation 1	Method 1	Method 2		
	Observations	Observations		
Variation 2	Method 1	Method 2	Method 1	
	Observations	Observations	Observations	
Variation 3	Method 1	Method 2	Method 1	Method 2
	Observations	Observations	Observations	Observations

As for the *true experiment* and the *quasi-experiment*, it is important to keep all other conditions apart from the method the same across the study when using a single-subject design. For example, you would ensure that the same teacher delivered all lessons and that all of the lessons were delivered in the morning or all were delivered in the afternoon. This consistency would help to ensure that any differences in the amount that the students write when the different methods are used is less likely to be affected by teacher factors or time of day. While you may find that there could be more data collection occasions within the same period, the amount of data collected on each occasion would be quite small. You will find other points that are also important to consider, but you may see either the single-subject experiment or the quasi-experiment as feasible. As with the other types of experiments, it is important to *ensure good alignment between the research question and the chosen research design.*

In summary, if you decide to use an experimental design for your small-scale study, you are least likely to conduct a true experiment and more likely to use a quasi-experiment or a single-subject design. This is because most educational research involves working with intact classes whose members cannot be separated for practical reasons. Circumstances rarely enable you to allocate participants randomly to control and experimental groups and change the composition of existing classes. If you decided to employ a quasi-experiment or a single-subject design, the other features of experiments would still be present—that is:

- *Quantitative data* would be collected.
- A *theory* would be *tested*.
- There would be an *intervention*.

- You would test whether the *independent variable* (the intervention) *caused a change in the dependent variable* (for example, the amount of words that students write).

Table 5.2 provides a summary comparison of the key features of true experiments, quasi-experiments and single-subject experiments.

Table 5.2 Summary comparison of experimental designs

	True experiment	Quasi-experiment	Single-subject experiment
Quantitative data	✓	✓	✓
Theory testing	✓	✓	✓
Intervention	✓	✓	✓
Cause and effect	✓	✓	✓
Random allocation	✓		

It is now time to think about which experimental design you would prefer if you were conducting research into the creative writing problem.

 For your notebook

Exercise 5.3 Which experimental design would you use for the creative writing problem?

Imagine that you were to design an experiment around the creative writing scenario. The design you choose would depend very much on the purpose of your research and you would develop a research question that complemented both your purpose and your chosen research design.

The situation is hypothetical and you have not conducted a literature review. Your theory will therefore also be hypothetical.

Briefly describe your problem and the context, changing and adding details to the scenario as you choose.

- What is the purpose of your research?
- What theory are you testing (mention the cause and the effect)?
- What is your intervention?
- What is your specific research question?
- Explain your sample (number of students, from where).
- What quantitative data will you collect?
- Which experimental design will you use?
- List reasons why you chose this particular experimental design.
- List reasons why you did not choose each of the other experimental designs.

Record your response as 'Exercise 5.3 Which experimental design would you use for the creative writing problem?'

Non-experiments

Quantitative research does not always involve conducting experiments to *predict* which methods of teaching, for example, are more effective than others. While researchers aim to be able to apply the findings from experiments to other similar groups or samples from the same *population* (or group from which the sample is chosen), sometimes their aim is simply to describe certain features of the sample of interest, at least as the starting point for their quantitative study. For example, they may wish to know how many words on average (the *mean* in statistical terms) that each child in the class writes during creative writing lessons and calculate the *percentage* of students in the class who wrote more than a certain number of words or less than a certain number of words. They may just want to know the status quo at first by using *descriptive statistics* such as means and percentages, but they will often want to use this information to go further. At that level, the results are really only of interest in the particular context, and it cannot be inferred that the findings can be applied to similar groups, but the question then would be why there is interest in simply describing an aspect of the situation in numerical terms and how the results can be useful.

It is more likely that descriptive statistics might be used for something like identifying which students write the least during creative writing lessons and then working with just one or two of those students, perhaps using a single-subject design. In this situation, the descriptive statistics are used for identifying one or more students who could be involved in the study. Rather than seeing these two steps as different phases in the study, they are likely to be seen as part of the same study or phase of the study because it is only after identifying the participants that the most useful part of the research can take place. As the main emphasis would be on the experimental part of this research, however, the research might not be regarded strictly as a non-experiment.

A common example of quantitative research that is non-experimental is *correlational research*, which cannot test for cause and effect. Instead, correlational research looks for *patterns of association* or *statistical correlation* between variables that are not manipulated. The underlying assumption in correlational research is that the design itself is *not capable of testing for cause and effect*. It is also not logical to be able to conclude from the particular variables involved that one variable could be capable of causing change in the other, but it does show that the two are related.

For example, it may be logical for a researcher to test whether there is a (statistical) correlation between gender and learning style preferences of students at the upper primary or upper elementary level, such that being male means that you are more likely to have a preference for one learning style and being female may mean that you are more likely to have a different preferred learning style. It would not be logical, however, to test whether having particular learning style preferences causes students to be male or female, or whether being male or female caused students to have particular learning style preferences. This is because students cannot be (randomly) allocated to gender or learning style preferences. Researchers therefore choose either experimental or correlational research designs based on underlying logic and whether the independent variables can be manipulated.

Creswell (2012) explains that there are two main types of *correlational designs*: those that *explain* the relationship between the variables (as is the case with the above example) and those that use variables (called *predictor variables*) that enable a future outcome to be predicted.

Returning to the creative writing scenario, we see an example of an *explanatory correlational design* in which two variables are measured at the same time: how much the students write and how much they enjoy the creative writing lessons. The researcher may hypothesise that there is a relationship (or correlation) between these two variables. The hypothesis may even anticipate the *direction* (positive or negative) and *strength* of the relationship, as explained below. The researcher would need to quantify the amount that students write and work out how to gauge students' levels of enjoyment in the lessons. How to measure variables such as these will be discussed in Chapter 5.

When the data are entered onto a spreadsheet in a statistical program and the calculations completed, the results will show whether there is a relationship between how much students write and their levels of enjoyment in the lessons. Perhaps the more students enjoy the lessons, the more they tend to write, and perhaps less enjoyment is associated with writing fewer words. When the scores on both variables go up or down together, the *direction* of the correlation is said to be *positive*. If enjoyment is low when the amount that students write is high or vice versa, however, the *direction* of the correlation is *negative*.

The *strength* of the correlation is described as *low, medium or high*, and depends on the final statistic, which will be somewhere between −1.0 and +1.0. Care needs to be taken not to imply or conclude that there is a causal relationship. It is also possible to find very little or no correlation between variables—that is, when neither positive nor negative correlations are evident.

In my research (see Example 3 from Chapter 1), I found a high positive correlation between pre-service teachers' confidence to solve mathematical problems and their confidence to teach others to solve mathematical problems. As the two variables were measured together, this part of my research used an explanatory correlational design. On the other hand, if confidence to teach mathematical problem solving at the pre-service teacher level was used to predict levels of confidence to teach mathematical problem solving to others following graduation, then the second variable would be measured later, when the pre-service teachers became practising teachers. Thus, in a correlational design that involves explanation, the variables are measured at the same time. In a correlational design that involves prediction, the measurement of the two variables is separated by time. If you decide that a correlational design is appropriate for your research, you would be unlikely to employ a prediction design because the timeframe would not suit your circumstances unless measurements on the predictor variable were taken previously and you had access to those results.

The following research question drafted for the scenario could provide a starting point for thinking about the relationship between enjoyment of the lessons and how much students write during their creative writing lessons: 'Do children who enjoy their creative writing lessons write significantly more than children who derive less enjoyment from their lessons?'

To conclude our thinking here, you could return to the criteria for writing good research questions discussed in Chapter 2 to take the question to later iterations. The final question, however, would depend on the researcher's theory, which is related to what was found in previous research in the area (from the literature review) and on logic. If you think your research question points you in the direction of quantitative research and perhaps correlational research design, it would be important to do further reading in the area, as indicated at the end of the chapter. Being able to argue why you chose one type of correlational design over another would help to make your argument for your chosen research design more convincing.

MIXED-METHODS RESEARCH DESIGNS: KEY FEATURES, USES AND LIMITATIONS

Mixed-methods research designs involve the collection of both quantitative and qualitative data, either *at or about the same time* or *one before the other*, in either order, depending on the purpose of the research and the research questions. Some mixed-methods research gives *similar or equal weighting* to quantitative and qualitative data, while other mixed-methods research gives *more emphasis to one over the other*. Whether the two types of data will be collected using *separate or the same methods*, how they *connect* with each other and how they are dealt with when analysing and reporting the findings of the study also need to be considered. While some mixed-methods designs are executed in a *single phase*, others need *several phases* to accommodate the different types of data collected and steps in the process. Creswell (2012) explains how the *timing*, the *weighting* and the *emphasis* determine the type of mixed-methods design used. He also defines mixed-methods designs as advanced procedures. While mixed methods may not be the most realistic design for first time or novice researchers, understanding something about how they can work in practice and what they can achieve helps to provide more perspective and understanding about the strengths and limitations of using either quantitative or qualitative designs.

When Louise evaluated her program for young parents and young prospective parents (see Example 1 in Chapter 1) she collected qualitative data from her parent participants using two different methods (both of which will be discussed in Chapter 6). There were two reasons for collecting the qualitative **survey** data prior to conducting the **focus group interview**. First, Louise used information from the individual surveys to select participants for her focus group interview who were quite different from each other and, as a

Survey A survey can be quantitative or qualitative (Punch, 2003), although a common misperception is that surveys are quantitative only and questionnaires are qualitative. Surveys can involve the collection of quantitative or qualitative data or a combination of both.

Focus group interview In focus groups, participants are generally invited to attend, and are encouraged by the interviewer to interact with each other rather than respond to the interviewer only.

group, more representative of the range of clients who completed the program than might have otherwise been the case. Second, the focus group interview enabled Louise to explore more deeply themes that had emerged from her initial analysis of the survey data. There were two specific research questions, one relating to the parents' perceptions of the content of the program and one relating to parents' perceptions of the delivery of the program in terms of meeting their needs. The survey and the focus group interview each addressed both research questions.

Louise could have constructed a number of questions on her survey that asked the parents to tick boxes to indicate the *extent* to which the content of the program and the delivery of the program met their needs. This would have provided Louise with *quantitative data*. The focus group interview would then enable her to explore the results and patterns evident from her analysis of the survey data. This approach would have meant that Louise collected quantitative data first, followed by *qualitative data*.

If Louise wanted to collect quantitative and qualitative data *at the same time*, she could have incorporated both types of questions into either the survey or the interview. She would then miss out on the opportunities that having the two methods of data collection provided her, and the opportunity to explore particular points that she may not have otherwise anticipated without analysing the quantitative data first. Yet another option would have been to explore aspects of the content and delivery of the program in the interview first, before asking the parents to complete the quantitative surveys individually; however, having parents complete the survey first had the advantage of capturing parents' individual responses before they shared their thoughts in an interview. Louise's decision to interview a smaller number of parents who completed the survey would need to be revisited when considering alternative ways to conduct her study. It appears that if Louise wanted to use a *mixed-methods design, the quantitative survey followed by the focus group interview would have been the more logical choice.*

Given that Louise's research questions were complementary and particularly because they were both qualitative rather than a combination of quantitative and qualitative, incorporating the two research questions into a small-scale study was achievable as well as logical. The project could have used a mixed-methods design, although in that case Louise would need to consider very seriously the feasibility of this approach for her. Learning about different quantitative and qualitative research methods (Chapter 6) and how to analyse both quantitative and qualitative data (Chapter 8) alone can be difficult for a student completing her first research project. On the other hand, Louise's literature review enabled her to develop a sound conceptual framework for her study, which was carried through to the design of the study and the methods chosen for data collection, and finally through to the presentation of her findings. When considering a mixed-methods design, Louise would revisit her literature review and also the methods used in previous studies. She would then be able to decide whether using a mixed-methods design would complement or extend approaches taken in previous research. The latter scenario could mean that her research could possibly make a contribution not only because of what she found but also through her choice of research design.

In further considering the feasibility of employing a mixed-methods design, Louise would think about the knowledge and skills that she would need to develop around aspects of quantitative research, such as learning how to *construct groups of questions or scales* for her survey to *measure* the extent to which the parents felt that the content and delivery of the program met their needs. She would need to take care, however, that she did not lose sight of the fact that the *evaluation* was to focus on the program, not on evaluating those delivering it.

Louise would also need to add to her learning *how to deal with and analyse quantitative data* and the *type of statistics* that would be appropriate. She might consider increasing her research questions from two to four, so that she could have one quantitative and one qualitative research question relating to the content of her program and one of each relating to the delivery of her program. Her additional research questions would need to indicate that quantitative data would be collected and could, for example, begin with 'To what extent'. Alternatively, she could address the quantitative and qualitative side in a single question for each of the two areas, although she would still need to be aware that her project would now strictly have four research questions for which she would have data that would need to be organised, analysed and then presented as findings in her written report of the project. She would need to learn how to *report both quantitative and qualitative findings* and the *language* appropriate to both, and she would also need to return to and reconsider the purpose of her research and her broad research question, again checking alignment between all of the parts. Deciding on the research design therefore has implications at each stage of the study, from the planning right through to the writing of the research report.

It may appear that my advice to Louise would be to stay with her qualitative design rather than to use a mixed-methods design, but it is important for novice and particularly first-time researchers with a restricted timeframe to consider the implications before making such decisions. Planning, conducting and reporting your first research project can represent a steep learning curve. If you can consider all of the options—quantitative, qualitative and mixed-methods designs—before making your decision, your overall learning will be a little broader and deeper than if you took the option that appealed initially. The philosophical approach mentioned earlier, where you consider each design as a possible contender for your research question/s, enables you to build a more convincing case for your final choice. It is probably also worth thinking of your early research projects as opportunities to begin learning about the research process and how to think systematically about challenges or what makes you curious. It is not about reaching ground-breaking conclusions that will have wide implications.

Novice researchers are often advised to focus on just one research question. The fact that Louise's research questions were complementary and both qualitative rather than a combination of qualitative and quantitative together helped to ensure that the project was achievable within her timeframe.

It is now time to think about your research project again. By this stage, your ideas probably point you in the direction of either a qualitative study or a quantitative study. Before making what might be some of your most likely final decisions, take a moment to imagine what your project could look like if you included both quantitative and qualitative data collection.

For your notebook

Exercise 5.4 What could my research look like if I used mixed methods?

First, provide the latest iterations of your topic, problem, broad research question, purpose statement and specific research questions. (You will also need this information for Exercise 5.6.)

Experiment with drawing a few diagrams to illustrate the different ways in which your research could be conducted if you used a mixed-methods design before deciding on which approach you would take if you used mixed methods. Consider:

- *Timing:* Will you collect your quantitative and qualitative data at the same time or one after the other? Why?

- *Sequencing:* If you collect qualitative and quantitative data one after the other, which one comes first and why?

- *Weighting:* Will you give equal weight to the collection of quantitative and qualitative data? If not, which will receive greater weighting and why?

- *Methods:* What methods will you use to collect your qualitative and quantitative data? Will you use the same methods for both or will you use different methods? What are the advantages and disadvantages of your choices?

Exercise 5.5 for your notebook invites you to revisit your notes and readings from your literature review and possibly to return directly to the articles that you reviewed to check whether any of the research reports fitted into one of the research designs discussed in this chapter. As mentioned in Chapter 4, we often return to the evidence-based research articles that we looked at earlier and read them for a different purpose. This is because we see things that we did not see before, and so the revisiting is well worthwhile, even if you conclude that you do not see any of the new points that you are currently learning. If you find case studies or realist or critical ethnographies, however, then you will have examples of how these studies are conducted and reported. Should you wish to continue your studies in research methods or decide to adopt an ethnographic design, most likely at a later stage, you will pursue further reading about these research designs.

 For your notebook

Exercise 5.5 What research designs were used in research reported in the articles in my literature review?

Revisit the notes that you took about each of the articles that you included in your literature review.

What research design was used in each study?

If your notes do not indicate the research design, revisit the article/s and check whether the authors identified the type of research design used. The abstract and the methods sections could be the first places to check in the articles.

If an article does not specifically note the research design used or refers more broadly to the design, such as a case study, working from your reading of this chapter and reading the relevant parts of the article again carefully, see whether you can determine more detail, such as the particular type of case study employed.

Draw up a table showing the articles that you used in your literature review and the research designs that each research project used.

Underneath your table, write a short paragraph to draw the information together, such as explaining whether all of the research used qualitative or quantitative designs and, if so, whether the balance was even or uneven, or whether mixed-methods research was used.

Now check in your literature review whether you mentioned the designs of the studies that you reviewed. Look for how you can include this information, even in passing, if it is not already there.

It is now time to make the big decision about which research design you will use for your small-scale study. Record your decision in the concluding exercise for this chapter.

CONCLUDING EXERCISE

 For your notebook

Exercise 5.6 Which research design is appropriate for my study?

Copy from Exercise 5.4 the information around your topic, problem, broad research question, purpose statement and specific research questions. Make any further refinements needed.

Record your choice of research design.

Argue why this particular design is most appropriate for your small-scale study:

- List the advantages and limitations of this design in relation to your research.

- Discuss other close contending designs and why you did not choose them.

- Explain why the other designs are unsuitable for your research.

CHAPTER SUMMARY

In this chapter, you took the time to:

- begin to learn about a range of qualitative and quantitative research designs and different approaches to mixed-methods research designs

- engage with a classroom scenario about the teaching of creative writing and how it could form the basis for thinking about different types of qualitative and quantitative research designs

- consider how Louise's qualitative research project could have been planned using a mixed-methods design

- think more deeply about your own research project ideas and re-examine your ideas in light of your developing understanding of qualitative, quantitative and mixed-methods research designs

- update your ideas for your own research, cementing your ideas about your choice of research design and ensuring that the key parts of the plan, including your topic, broad research question, the purpose of your research, your statements about why your research is important and to whom, and your choice of research design are all in alignment

- consider the implications of your choice of research design in terms of your timeframe, your course or subject requirements, and your personal circumstances

- read definitions of important key terms: action research, case, correlation, deductive analysis, dependent variable, ethnography, experiment, focus group interview, independent variable, inductive analysis, instrumental case study, multiple case study, quasi-experiment, survey, theory building, theory testing.

TAKING IT FURTHER

> Now that you have been introduced to a number of qualitative and quantitative and mixed-methods designs and made your decision about which approach you will most likely take with your small-scale research project, select some reading below to take your learning further with your chosen design.

FURTHER READING

Bell, J. (2010), *Doing Your Research Project: A guide for first-time researchers in education, health and social sciences* (5th ed.), Maidenhead: Open University Press.
See Chapter 1.

Creswell, J.W. (2012), *Educational Research: Planning, conducting and evaluating quantitative or qualitative research* (4th ed.), Boston: Pearson Education.
Select the chapter corresponding to your chosen design.

McMillan, J.H. & Schumacher, S. (2010), *Research in Education: Evidence-based inquiry* (7th ed.), Upper Saddle River, NJ: Pearson Education.
See Chapter 10 or Chapter 11, as appropriate.

McMillan, J.H. & Wergin, J.F. (2010), *Understanding and Evaluating Educational Research* (4th ed.), Boston: Pearson Education.
See Chapter 1.

Punch, K.F. & Oancea, A. (2014), *Introduction to Research Methods in Education* (2nd ed.), London: Sage.
See Chapter 8 on qualitative research or Chapter 11 on quantitative research as appropriate.

6

Research methods

This chapter will help you to:

 understand several commonly used methods for collecting quantitative or qualitative data

 choose your data-collection methods for your small-scale study based on your research question/s.

Imagine stepping out of your front door (real or virtual) on your first day of data collection. Will you know where to go and who to see? Will you know what to do when you get to your destination? The first question relates to choosing the *location and participants* for your study. The second question relates to knowing about different *methods of data collection* (for example, surveys, interviews and observations), choosing and justifying one or more methods and *data collection instruments* appropriate for your problem and your research questions. It also involves preparing and trialling your data-collection instruments (such as surveys, interview guides or observation schedules) and the way that you collect your data (for example by administering surveys, conducting interviews or making observations). Many decisions and preparations therefore need to be made relating to your *research methods* before your first day of data collection.

As you work through this chapter and think about selecting the location, participants and your method/s of data collection or generation and preparing your research instruments, keep beside you the ideas that you developed around your topic, problem, broad research question, the purpose of your study, specific research question/s and research design. You should continue to toggle back and forth between all of these parts as you make choices about your methods. The iterative process of developing and refining your research questions continues, and you may even make final adjustments to your research questions or other parts of your developing plans by the end of this chapter and after reading other relevant literature.

This chapter partly extends on some of the practical and ethical considerations regarding your methods that were the focus of Chapter 3. Before you put forward a research proposal, apply for ethical clearance to conduct your research or commence your data collection, it is also important to consider how your data will be analysed (Chapter 8).

PARTICIPANTS AND SAMPLING

Choosing the location and participants are two of the most important decisions that you will make when planning your research. Specific research questions should indicate the intended participants. In early iterations of research questions, novice researchers may identify their participants as 'Australian students' or 'Canadian students', for example. Such a broad sweep would mean all students at all year or grade levels, in all educational institutions across the country.

The next step is to narrow the focus. Data cannot be collected from all students, or even *representative samples* or *random samples* of all categories of students across the country in a small-scale study. One way to narrow the focus is to choose a category that is logical and achievable. This may lead you to, for example, a Year 5 class in a small, rural, public school in your state or province. Identifying a narrower category of participants helps with developing questions in a survey or interview, for example, that are suitable for the year level, reading levels and experience if the participants are students. To identify a particular *sample* of students from the Year 5 *population* in the state or province that is appropriate for your small-scale study, you need to understand different sampling techniques.

Novice researchers conducting small-scale studies will often choose their participants not just because they are appropriate for the *purpose* of the research but because of convenience. *Convenience samples* can be realistic in terms of access and time. For example, it may be possible to choose participants who are located in a school near you. Describing the sample and the demographics carefully in the methods section of the research report (without identifying the school) is important, because it gives meaning and context to the findings of the study and how they can be interpreted, and colleagues in similar contexts could see parallels with their contexts or situations and consider the findings when reflecting on their own practice and professional circumstances.

Experienced researchers undertaking larger-scale studies may have a wider range of sampling options than researchers who need to keep their research small-scale and manageable.

For your notebook

Exercise 6.1 Thinking about your sample

Think about the purpose of your small-scale study and identify the characteristics that you would need to look for in your participants.

- How and where do you think that you could identify a suitable sample?

- Check your ideas about your sample against your research questions.

- Make refinements to your research question/s if needed.

Put these notes to one side, labelling them 'Exercise 6.1 Thinking about your sample'. You can return to these notes periodically throughout the chapter, making adjustments as appropriate as you begin to learn about surveys or questionnaires and achievement tests, interviews and observations as commonly used methods of collecting or generating data.

SURVEYS/QUESTIONNAIRES AND TESTS

It is not always easy to appreciate how difficult or time-consuming it can be to develop surveys or questionnaires and tests for collecting data. Surveys (quantitative, qualitative and mixed-methods) and tests (for example, achievement tests) need to appear simple and easy to navigate, even though these traits can mask the effort that went into their construction. Respondents should be able to focus their attention on deciding on their responses rather than on how to interpret the questions that are asked. Questions or items on surveys and tests therefore need to be:

- easy to understand by the range of people who complete them
- capable of being interpreted by all respondents in the same way
- interpreted in the way intended by the person who constructed them.

The task of constructing surveys can also appear simple because surveys are so common in everyday life. The above points are very important for ensuring that the responses that people give faithfully answer the questions intended and the survey as a whole addresses the research question/s in the study.

Ease and speed of administration of surveys are often-quoted justifications provided by novice research students for choosing surveys as methods of data collection. Designing surveys is quite complex, however. The areas to consider can be divided into six groups:

1. conceptual framework and definition of variables
2. construction of the questions or items for each variable
3. response format and physical presentation of the questions
4. pilot testing
5. administration of the survey, and
6. organisation of data and data entry and analysis.

All these areas apply to quantitative, qualitative and mixed-methods surveys. The only real variations relate to the wording of the questions, the response format, and the data entry and analysis. As Punch (2003) points out, the same logic underlies the approach to both quantitative and qualitative surveys, and having an understanding of how to approach quantitative surveys therefore helps with learning how to construct good qualitative surveys. Sometimes researchers use pre-existing surveys or tests (with permission as appropriate), but often they need to construct their own so that the instruments address their specific research questions and are appropriate for their participants.

Conceptual framework and definition of variables

All three examples of research projects presented in Chapter 1 (Louise's evaluation of her program for young and prospective young parents, Maria's interest in how pre-service teachers can engage with and teach Aboriginal students and my research into pre-service teachers' levels of self-efficacy for solving mathematical problems and teaching others to solve mathematical problems) had *conceptual frameworks* with elements that were both distinct and interrelated. These elements were reflected in the research questions, research designs and methods of data collection and presentation of findings. Louise's data, collected through *qualitative surveys* and a *focus group interview*, related to the *content* and *delivery* of her program, as perceived by the young parents; Maria collected data in the form of qualitative surveys that enabled the pre-service teachers to articulate what they were learning with regard to engaging with and teaching Aboriginal students; and my quantitative surveys asked pre-service teachers to indicate how confident they were in solving problems across a range of mathematical operations and how confident they were to teach others to solve mathematical problems in the same areas. In each case, the elements of the conceptual framework were rooted in critiques of evidence-based research literature and the research questions, while the surveys or questionnaires directly addressed the same elements. This meant that the researchers were able to report the findings under each of the research questions.

It is important to use the conceptual framework as a broad structure for the survey, especially if the survey is the only method of data collection used. If there is more than one method of data collection, then the researcher considers how the elements or different parts of the conceptual framework are articulated across the different methods.

Underpinning the questions on the survey is a *clear definition of the key variables*, so that the focus of the questions infers the researcher's understanding of the variables to be *explored* (in the case of qualitative research) or *measured* (in quantitative research). For example, self-efficacy refers to how confident a person is to complete *specific tasks* successfully in the future. The *questions or items* on the survey therefore need to reflect the definition of self-efficacy established in the literature by referring to *specific* mathematical operations to allow differences or similarities in levels of self-efficacy across those areas to be identified.

The following tables and accompanying explanations illustrate one way of beginning with an over-arching conceptual framework, breaking down its component parts and then developing items on a quantitative survey. The same general approach can be taken when devising qualitative surveys to explore variables of interest or when developing achievement tests that reflect the work covered in a particular subject area in class during the period over which the research is conducted.

Table 6.1 is a matrix that summarises the broad structure of the survey I developed. The conceptual framework has two over-arching concepts: self-efficacy to solve mathematical problems and self-efficacy to teach others to solve mathematical problems. The six scales in the first column each contained between 4 and 10 questions or items in each of the two areas (Columns 2 and 3), with each item in one area having a matching item in the other area, as will be illustrated in Table 6.2.

Table 6.1 Example of a matrix to guide the development of a survey

Conceptual framework		
Mathematical scales	Self-efficacy to solve mathematical problems	Self-efficacy to teach others to solve mathematical problems
Concepts	10 items	10 items
Number	8 items	8 items
Measurement	10 items	10 items
Fractions	5 items	5 items
Space	4 items	4 items
Chance and data	7 items	7 items

Table 6.2 shows the four items corresponding to the scale for space, illustrating how the items enabled self-efficacy to be tested at the specific as opposed to general level, which is consistent with self-efficacy theory. Respondents were asked to place a check in the appropriate square for each of the four items.

Table 6.2 Items on the scale for space

How confident are you in **solving spatial problems**, including the following:

Concept	1	2	3	4	5	6
Faces						
Edges						
Vertices						
Triangles						

Key

1 = Not very confident at all
2 = Only just confident
3 = Reasonably confident
4 = Very confident
5 = Extra confident
6 = Super confident

The same questions were then asked with reference to teaching others to solve spatial problems. This meant that the same four items were asked in relation to space for each of the two areas in the conceptual framework. The same pattern was followed for each of the other five mathematical scales listed in Column 1 of the matrix (Table 6.1).

It was *hypothesised* before the data were collected that there would be a high positive *correlation* between the responses on the two sets of scales (self-efficacy to solve mathematical problems and self-efficacy to teach others to solve mathematical problems in each area of mathematics). This meant that it was predicted that pre-service teachers who had high levels of self-efficacy to solve problems in any of mathematical areas listed in Table 6.1, for example, would also have high levels of self-efficacy to teach others to solve problems in these same areas. The same pattern was predicted for low levels of self-efficacy.

If you need to construct a survey or test, your matrix to guide the development of your instrument will take into account your own conceptual framework. You may have fewer scales to develop—for example, if your participants are children and your research is focused on their learning in one sub-area over a short period, such as several weeks, or if your instrument is qualitative. In the latter case, you may have fewer items in each area because your respondents may need more time to develop their responses in words.

Construction of the questions (or items)

The following criteria for developing good survey questions need to be followed:

- *Be clear and simple*, avoiding complex terms or terms that may not be understood or could be understood differently by different respondents. For example, I would not use the term 'self-efficacy' in a survey because it has a very technical meaning that is unlikely to be known by or shared among the participants. I could provide a definition but it is more straightforward to avoid technical terms if possible. If constructing achievement tests, the terminology and the content will reflect the teaching over the period of interest. Questions that are clear also *avoid double negatives*.
- *Focus on one point only per item*. Double-barrelled questions need to be rewritten as two separate questions, otherwise it is often not possible to determine which of the two questions respondents answered when there is only provision for a single response. You may need a response to both questions.
- *Avoid assumptions*. For example, we would not ask respondents to indicate the extent to which boys are more confident than girls because the assumption may not be *valid*. Some areas are very complex and cannot be reduced to broad statements.
- *Avoid bias*. Bias could occur, for example, if asking respondents to indicate the extent to which they think that each of a number of factors impacts on why

students in one schooling system receive an education that is superior to the education that students receive in another system. Such bias has inherent *ethical issues*.

- *Avoid asking too many questions*, as this can lead to insufficient attention being given to responding because of fatigue or trying to complete the survey within a limited timeframe. Consider the age of the respondents and their concentration spans, and also whether a survey is the best or only way to gain the information that you require from your participants.

- *Ask several questions in each specific area.* For example, with quantitative surveys we need at least three or four well-constructed questions in a specific area to establish *reliable* measures of participants' thoughts. In some cases, we need to construct a greater number of questions at first so that we can eliminate any that are not working well or cannot be fixed. A single question could be quite 'hit and miss'.

- *Avoid asking questions 'just in case'* the responses may be helpful. It may be important to ask some questions at the beginning of the survey for the purpose of organising data, but it is not *ethical* or *efficient* to ask participants for personal information, such as their age, unless it is critical to the research or important for addressing the research question.

Response format and physical presentation of the questions
Researchers can use several different options for survey response formats. One option for quantitative surveys, which is shown in Table 6.2, is to provide boxes that can be checked against each question or item and according to where on the scale (presented at the top) respondents see themselves

as falling. Notice that there are six options along the top (response format) and each has a descriptor under the key, which I placed at the side. The descriptors were very important: I needed to find descriptors that not only appeared on a scale from 'Not very confident at all' to 'Super confident', but I had to check that these descriptors were likely to be understood by the respondents in the same way that I understood them.

I decided that I wanted an even response format, which meant that there was no mid-point that could be checked as an easy option. Instead, I wanted the participants to think more deeply about their responses. I found from my previous research in the area that pre-service teachers were able to differentiate the finer distinctions that a six-point scale provided, although I have also used a four-point response format, especially when working with children around the ages of nine or ten years.

Many quantitative surveys use an uneven response format. Each survey needs to be considered independently when making the choice of response format and researchers need to think about the consequences of their choices. They also need to consider that young children may find it easier to select from printed icons, such as facial expressions, and may need to have the questions read to them. If the children are very young, a different method of data collection or data generation could be more appropriate.

Each item on the survey could also be separated physically. Showing the response format at the top once only for each set of items, however, was simpler for me, tightened the appearance and made the survey appear less onerous to complete. I ensured that all items in each set appeared on the same page, avoiding the need for participants to work across two pages while responding to single sets of items.

When the wording associated with each numeral on the

scale in the response format is very short, it is often possible to put the wording at the top rather than to use a key at the side. Another approach is to have a larger number of options, for example from 1 to 10, providing descriptors for the lowest and highest options only. This can work as long as the piloting of the survey shows that making choices in between the extremes and with a larger number of options is realistic and achievable for potential participants.

It is also important to examine other response formats and other ways of presenting the questions on a survey, including quantitative and qualitative surveys or surveys that use mixed methods.

 For your notebook

Exercise 6.2 What can quantitative, qualitative and mixed-methods surveys look like?

Have a look around to see what surveys you can find— for example, in magazines, at home, in your workplace, at university, in shopping centres or online. The surveys may reach you via mail, email or be handed to you in person. Find both quantitative and qualitative surveys. Also see whether you can find examples that collect both quantitative and qualitative data, with the latter often providing space for written responses.

Lay the examples out on the table in front of you, separating the quantitative, qualitative and mixed-methods surveys. Make comparisons between:

- their presentation
- the instructions that they give
- the personal or demographic details that they ask (usually at the start)

- the type of questions asked

- the response formats (how many options, even or uneven format, whether or how many descriptors were used for quantitative survey items) and the general layout for responses on qualitative items

- the number of different sections that each survey contains and/or the number of items

- the number of pages and whether both sides of the page are used if the survey is paper based (this makes the survey appear more compact)

- other points, such as whether there is a thank you note at the top or bottom of the survey.

 For your notebook

Exercise 6.3 What could your survey look like?

Returning to your research question and thinking about the conceptual framework that provides the structure for your research and your literature review, consider whether you could use a survey as one of your research methods for your small-scale study. If you use a survey, will it gather quantitative data or generate or collect qualitative data or a mixture of both?

- Draft a matrix similar to Table 6.1 before drafting your questions for your survey. Then experiment with different ways of presenting your questions and different response formats, based on those that you have seen, characteristics of your potential participants (such as whether they are children and how young) as well as your imagination and what seems logical to you. Construct the first draft of your quantitative, qualitative or mixed-methods survey.

- Write the instructions for completing the survey.

You may find inspiration online from SurveyMonkey as well as from among the examples of surveys found when completing Exercise 6.2 in your notebook.

Pilot testing

It is now time to see what others think of the first draft of your survey, and to get them to provide feedback and suggestions that you might incorporate into the next draft of your survey (quantitative, qualitative or mixed methods).

 For your notebook

Exercise 6.4 What do others think of your survey?

Gather a small group of fellow students or colleagues who are willing to look at your survey independently at first, before taking part in a discussion that you facilitate.

Without providing any additional explanations, ask your colleagues to read the instructions and complete your draft survey individually.

Note the amount of time taken by each person to complete the survey. (This will help you to estimate how much time the participants in your study will need to complete your survey.)

- Taking each question on your survey one at a time, ask each person to explain to the group what he or she *understood* by the item.

- Discuss any *differences in interpretations* with the group and explain what you meant by items that were unclear or not interpreted in the same way by each person.

- *Encourage interaction* between members of the group about how to improve the clarity of each item as necessary, referring to the characteristics of your potential participants.

- Repeat the above steps, focusing on the *instructions* at the top of the survey.

- Ask members to comment on the *presentation* of the survey and how it could be improved.

- *Tidy the appearance of your survey*, making changes and refinements that resulted from the discussion.

- You might like to show a 'clean' copy to the group or to others for further comment.

Record the latest iteration of your survey as 'Exercise 6.4 What do others think of your survey?'

If your survey is a quantitative one, it will be important to trial or pilot test it with a large group of people with similar characteristics to the potential participants in your research to find out how well the items are working individually and collectively by assessing the *reliabilities* of the sets of items. Sometimes this occurs as a separate exercise before the main part of the research commences, and sometimes it occurs after the administration of the survey to the research participants. It involves recording the responses from each participant for each item and completing certain statistical operations. Further reading is suggested at the end of this chapter for taking your learning deeper and further if you intend to construct a quantitative survey.

Administration and collection of completed surveys

A number of decisions need to be made about the administration and collection of your surveys. You may be able to add to the following list.

Will your survey:

- be online or paper-based?
- be supervised (for example with a class) or unsupervised?
- be administered by you (or another person)?
- involve children? If so, consider whether you will leave it to the children to complete the survey without further input from you after you explain the exercise. Alternatively, perhaps it will involve you reading each question aloud, providing time for students to complete each question before you read the next one. (This procedure can be used with children so that they all start and finish the survey together and the papers are collected from everyone at the same time. This approach may make the procedures simpler and also help to ensure that reading ability does not impact ability to respond.) It is also often helpful to have children double-check that all questions are answered before you collect their papers. Online surveys can also incorporate a check for completion of all items.
- be mailed to participants? If so, think about how you will collect the completed surveys, the timeline you will allow for the return of the surveys, and whether, how and when to remind non-respondents.

 For your notebook

Exercise 6.5 Administration and collection of your completed surveys

If you plan to use a survey to collect data, think through the options for the administration and collection of the survey, taking into account:

- characteristics of your participants (for example, whether they are children or adults)
- your location and the location of your participants
- what option you are most likely to use and why.

Record your responses in your notebook.

INTERVIEWS

Interviews will often follow surveys if more than one method of data collection is used. They provide the opportunity to explore some of the issues further—for example, why pre-service teachers might be more confident solving some types of mathematical problems than others.

In other research, interviews could be conducted first or they could be the only method of data collection. Deciding on what questions will be asked and even how the interviews will be conducted is usually more complex and difficult than is often imagined. Teachers are very familiar with asking questions—they ask many questions every day—but sometimes the idea of conducting interviews for their research is more challenging.

Students conducting small-scale studies are often required to begin to learn the process of conducting interviews by trialling their questions and their technique for conducting interviews with colleagues or fellow students, and even finding out how to analyse the data and present the findings. These are very valuable opportunities. It is a bit like pre-service teachers practising lessons on their fellow students or friends before reflecting on their lessons and delivering them to children for the first time. Just like teachers delivering lessons, researchers need to be very familiar with the questions that they will ask and how they will conduct their interviews, including welcoming participants and wrapping up the interview. Like a lesson, the start and finish are just as important as the middle.

Now that you are aware of the importance of these points, you can observe how others conduct interviews. There are many examples on television. They are often used in documentaries or in films, news reports or other broadcasts. You will see a wide variety of types of interviews and techniques for conducting them.

Interviews are often categorised as *individual, group* or *focus group*, and they can be *structured, semi–structured* or *unstructured*. Each has its own characteristics, such as how the questions are phrased, and each has strengths and limitations that need to be considered when deciding the *type of interview* that is suitable for the research questions and purpose of the study as well as for the people being interviewed. There are practical points to identify and think through around:

- planning and preparing for the interview (including the questions to ask)
- respecting interviewees and avoiding bias
- your tone of voice, how to respond to answers that are provided and your facial expressions and other gestures
- interviewee characteristics (such as whether the participants are children or adults)
- recording of interviews, transcripts and **member checking**

Member checking
This involves providing opportunities for interviewees to read through the transcripts of their interviews to check for accuracy or for anything that they would like changed or removed before the transcripts are finalised for analysis. Researchers decide in advance whether member checking will be part of their approach. It may also depend on how many people will be interviewed and the researcher's timeframe.

- the length of time taken to complete interviews
- conducting a trial to help refine your questions and your interview technique.

Types of interviews

The choice of *structured, semi-structured or unstructured interviews*, as well as whether the interviews will be conducted with *individuals or in groups*, can vary according to the *purpose* and *focus* of the research as well as *interviewee characteristics*. The researcher decides what needs to be found out or explored and then constructs an interview guide that includes the list of questions to be asked, reflecting the type of interview chosen. The responses could provide quantitative and/or qualitative data.

- *Closed questions* are suited to *structured interviews* and are asked as they are written on the page. The interviewer may tick boxes, for example, as the interviewee responds.
- *Semi-structured interviews* consist of *key questions* that the researcher plans in advance. The researcher can also explore interviewees' thoughts more deeply by asking complementary questions that are relevant at the time to encourage interviewees to expand on their responses. Complementary questions could include, for example, 'Would you like to tell me a bit more about that?' After planning the key questions, researchers try to anticipate possible complementary questions and prompts, and sometimes even write ideas down in advance. There is a little bit of thinking to do during the interview about how exactly these complementary or additional questions

will be asked if needed, while keeping the purpose or research questions in mind. Some researchers place their research questions at the top of the interview schedule to help them maintain focus throughout the interview, know when to ask for more information in an area and know when to continue with the next key question.

- Experienced researchers are more likely than novice researchers to use *unstructured interviews* when they have a general research question or general area that they wish to explore with interviewees. Interview questions are not prepared in advance. Analysing the interview transcripts can be more complex because the key themes need to be identified by examining the data rather than examining predetermined key themes that were deliberatively explored and will be present in the data.

If the purpose is to obtain *factual information* only, then the interview is more likely to be *structured*; if also wanting to include the opportunity to *explore issues more deeply*, then the *semi-structured interview* is likely to be more appropriate. Novice researchers are least likely to use the unstructured interview. This is partly because focusing on a topic that enables them to develop specific research questions, which are then used to guide the development of interview questions that address the specific research questions, is a 'safer' option for novice researchers. It helps the researcher to maintain a clear focus while planning, conducting and reporting the research, and to ensure that the study is small-scale and can be completed within the specified timeframe.

For illustrative purposes, we could return to the research question: 'What methods do exemplary teachers use to teach creative writing?'

If you knew which methods of teaching were options, then you could simply present different methods and ask which of them the exemplary teachers used and how they used them during creative writing lessons. This could be achieved during a structured interview. The problem might be whether the information received would be very informative or useful—or even logical. For example, the situation is much more complex than being able to conclude which methods teachers should use if they wish to be exemplary teachers of creative writing. Exemplary teachers (however they are defined) are likely to need to qualify their answers, which would be possible using a semi-structured interview. Such interviews could also enable the interviewees to identify and explain the methods that they use rather than simply to respond to whether and how they used methods that were proposed to them.

On the other hand, the researcher might be more interested in *how* teachers of creative writing *become exemplary*. The researcher may argue that it is necessary to remove the preconceived idea that it is the methods that are used that predominantly determine whether a teacher is exemplary and may even refine the research question. The researcher might opt for an interview that enables individual teachers to tell their career stories and to reflect on their teaching journeys. *Unstructured, individual interviews* could be used to explore the details of the stories as they *probe a number of aspects of the stories* that arise during their telling. The analyses of the interviews would then need to find their own ways forward in seeking answers to the research question rather than to structure the findings around specific, predetermined themes.

The unstructured interview could be longer than its structured and even semi-structured counterparts to enable the researcher and the participant to explore areas that arise, and the data analysis would probably also take longer. This is also one reason why unstructured interviews could be conducted *individually*: adequate time needs to be available for each interviewee to tell his or her story.

It could also be appropriate for teachers to bring to their interviews documents (or other artefacts) that they feel help them to illustrate certain points in their stories. For example, they might choose to bring a letter that influenced their career choice or sample lesson plans. There are many different types of documents that they could use. In some cases, it could be helpful for the researcher to have an understanding of the documents (such as syllabus documents); however, research focused primarily on analysing documents rather than the people who use the documents is a different type of research and not part of our discussion here.

The alternatives to individual interviews are *group* and *focus group interviews*. Interaction occurs between the interviewer and individual interviewees during group interviews, whereas in focus group interviews the researcher encourages interaction between the interviewees and guides the overall discussion of the questions that the interviewer asks. The aim of the focus group interview is not to seek consensus between those being interviewed but to enable the interaction between the interviewees to expose and explore differences as well as similarities between their ideas. The researcher needs to be skilled at deciding when and how to steer the discussion back to the key questions being asked and how to encourage all participants to express their ideas and views.

Interviewing children or members of other vulnerable groups, including some groups of adults, can carry higher levels of risk than interviewing adults who are not members of vulnerable groups. It would be helpful to return to the discussion around this point in Chapter 3, where we briefly considered implications around interviewing children, before discussing this point further with your lecturer or research supervisor if you think that your research could involve talking with children.

Each type of interview also requires researchers to be able to pace their way through the interview so that the interview finishes at a predetermined time known by all in advance, and ensures that all questions on the interview guide are addressed and appropriate weighting is given to each area under discussion.

Practical considerations

Apart from devising a list of questions for the interview, the researcher needs to step through each part of the interview ahead of time, *planning* how to commence the interview and how to help interviewees feel at ease, *preparing* information to provide at the start and deciding how to close the interview. It is commonplace to ask a final question that invites participants to add any other information that they believe could be relevant but that has not yet been covered. This could lead to a few more follow-up questions and responses. *Respecting interviewees* and their culture, as well as the time and consideration that they invest by being involved, and thanking them for their participation are all important. Interviewers also need to put their own ideas to the side and to *listen respectfully, avoid bias* and *be pleasant yet impartial*, so that some types of responses are not seen as being more appropriate than others. Children, in particular, may look for signs as to what types of answers will please you, whereas you are really interested in what they have to say, regardless of whether you agree with or like their ideas.

Should you wish to *record the interviews* (via audio or video), you can only do this if the participants (and guardians, where appropriate) agree. If either the participants or their guardians are not comfortable with the idea or would prefer that you did not record the interview, then that preference needs to be respected. Interviewees should know before they arrive at the interview whether it will be recorded, as you will have asked them about this earlier. It is also advisable to do a brief sound check just prior to commencing the interview. I also prefer to have a spare recording device and extra batteries when audio-recording interviews.

Recording interviews can have a number of advantages. It enables the researcher to focus on asking the questions, listening to responses and attending to the participants rather than being diverted by the need to write responses. If a smart pen or similar device is used to record the interview, the researcher can use a special pad to notate when each new question starts. For example, if the questions on the interview guide are numbered, the number of the question can be written on the special paper with the smart pen as each question is asked. When listening to the recording, the pen is placed where the number for a particular question is written. The pen will then take the recording back to where the question was asked.

Recording interviews also means that you can transcribe the text word for word as a *transcript*. Apart from being less reliant on memory and able to focus more on other important points during the interview, recording and completing transcripts mean that *member checking* can occur if arranged. The interviewees can have the opportunity to review transcripts of their interviews and make changes or deletions if appropriate. My advice is for novice researchers to complete their own transcripts rather than asking someone else to do them. Apart from needing to consider any possible *ethical implications* (discussed in Chapter 3), completing your own transcripts is important because it is a stage in the *data analysis*. As you complete the transcripts, you will pause the recording device frequently so that you can write each word down verbatim. You can also take the opportunity to note any initial points that could be important for the analysis.

It is also wise to consider the *length of the interview* ahead of time and take into account whether the participants are children or adults. The age of the children will help you to determine the maximum amount of time that you should set aside for the interview, beyond which time the interview is likely to be less productive. Adults are usually very busy people and part of respecting their contribution includes not taking any longer than is necessary.

It is recommended that you conduct a *trial* of your interview in advance of your data collection commencing. A trial has several advantages. You can:

- record the trial interview to check that your recorder is working and to help with your reflection
- determine whether your questions are well constructed and easily understood in the way that you intended them to be, or need modification
- time the interview and ensure that the maximum anticipated time (which you communicate to interviewees in advance) is not exceeded

- practise and reflect on your technique for conducting interviews and make adjustments for next time
- do a trial run of the data analysis, using data-analysis techniques that you identify in advance and even write up the trial so that you can hone your academic writing skills.

It is also very helpful if you can *reflect on the questions* (and their wording) as well as your *interview technique* with the *participants in your trial* of your interview when the trial interview is complete. Asking your colleagues (or people who have similar characteristics to those whom you will interview) to take part in a reflection after the trial can enable you to make the most of the trial by further refining the questions on your interview guide and getting feedback about your interview technique. While it may not always be possible to involve in the trial people who are very similar to the ones whom you will interview in your study, the wisdom and ability of colleagues who participate in your trial can make the effort very worthwhile. Sometimes, trial participants may raise points that might not otherwise be raised. The main point is that a trial is very useful—particularly for novice researchers.

 For your notebook

Exercise 6.6 Will you use an interview to collect data?

Consider whether you could conduct interviews to collect data for your small-scale study, based on your topic, broad research questions, purpose and specific research question/s as well as the location of your study and characteristics of your participants. Refer to your conceptual framework and other plans already made.

- What type of interview would be most appropriate and why? Consider whether your interview/s will be structured, semi-structured or unstructured, and individual, group or focus group. Note points for and against each option and justify your choices.

- What practical issues need to be considered and what practical decisions will you make?

- Draft your interview questions.

- When appropriate, trial your interview questions with several classmates or colleagues. Reflect on and refine your questions and note points for improving your technique.

OBSERVATIONS

Observations can also provide quantitative and/or qualitative data. Research involving observations has a long history of each of these approaches. Some approaches involve making observations while not participating in the action; others involve participating as well as observing. Key to deciding on the type of observation chosen is what you want to find out or establish, how your presence could affect the behaviours of those being observed and how observations could complement another method of data collection, such as interviews.

Some of my research included observing teachers and students during lessons. These observations enabled me to *establish and report* on the extent to which elements that defined the learning environments of interest were present during my *quasi-experimental* study. It was important for me to provide this evidence because the purpose of my research was to draw conclusions about levels of achievement and self-efficacy evident when these environments were used.

I developed a schedule for recording the extent to which the elements that defined the different environments were present in a selection of lessons that I videotaped. Rather than present this information on tables, I presented it as three-dimensional graphs that depicted for each learning environment the percentage of time that each defining element was observed throughout the periods of observation. Had I been interested in exploring teachers' and/or students' thoughts about working in these environments, however, I may have used the evidence from the observations as starting points for interviews.

Observations and observation schedules have a long history in classroom research. They have been used to find, for example, the relative percentages of time that teachers interact with boys and girls during lessons or the amount of class time devoted to teacher and student talk, respectively. The amount of time teachers spend dominating classroom talk can be surprisingly different from the amount of time for which teachers think they talk.

As with interviews and surveys, it is recommended that researchers who include observations and observation schedules in their studies trial their instruments (their observation schedules) and their use of them prior to the main stage of the study commencing. It is a good idea to focus the trial on *real-time observations or recordings*, depending on the intended method of undertaking the observations. If real-time observations are planned, then the initial training and practice in taking observations can also occur using recordings before practising in real time. This training or practice also concentrates on the extent to which the observations are *reliable*, and this can be addressed by comparing the observations recorded by different observers in the same context and at the same time. Practice

Inter-rater reliability
The degree of agreement or consensus among observers.

may be needed to increase what is referred to here as **inter-rater reliability**. When present to a high degree, such reliability builds confidence in both the method and the accuracy of the observations made (even by a single observer involved in the trial) and the conclusions reached in that regard.

It should also be remembered that observations—particularly when making video recordings of participants—carry a number of ethical issues and possibly dilemmas that need to be considered carefully and that may ultimately affect whether the research takes this direction.

Observations of participants do not necessarily always involve identifying in advance behaviours that will be observed, noted and quantified. As with all methods of collecting or generating data, such decisions depend on the research question and the purpose of the research, how previous research in the area was conducted, whether the research is focused on testing theory, on building theory or perhaps contributing to existing theory, and knowledge of the context in which the observations will be made.

Returning to the ideas about exploring the practice of exemplary teachers, and especially inviting the teachers to tell their stories, it could be appropriate for the researcher to *observe* an exemplary teacher in action. If, during the interview, the teacher refers to something that he or she did while being observed and to illustrate a point, the researcher and the participant have a similar reference point that could be helpful during the interview. It is quite common for interviews to follow on from observations. Observations on their own do not provide the opportunity to find out from those who were observed their interpretation of events or to explore why certain actions were taken. They can, however, be helpful in identifying points of interest that are further explored in an interview.

CHOOSING YOUR METHODS OF DATA COLLECTION

Your choice of data collection methods is based on the purpose of your research and your research questions, your knowledge of different methods and the methods used in previous research in your area of interest and the intended scale of your study. The next exercise for your notebook picks up on the last two points.

 For your notebook

Exercise 6.7 Reviewing your notes

At the beginning of the chapter, we imagined stepping out of the front door (real or virtual) on your first day of data collection and asked the following questions:

- Will you know where to go and who to see?
- Will you know what to do when you get to your destination?

Take each of these questions separately and make notes to show your current thoughts in regard to your study.

How do your responses fit in with your topic, problem and research questions?

For your notebook

Exercise 6.8 Which method/s of data collection will you use?

Return to the notes that you took while reading the evidence-based research articles in your area of interest regarding the research designs and method/s of data collection used for each study. Look at how the methods chosen related to the purpose of the research and the research questions.

Now revisit your own research question/s, the purpose of your study and other notes that you made—for example, around the design of your study.

Which method/s of data collection will you use? Are they the same or different from the methods used in previous research in your area? Why?

Note points to argue for your choices, remembering that your study is small-scale and needs to conform to the requirements of your course or subject.

CHAPTER SUMMARY

In this chapter, you took the time to:

- consider who your participants for your study might be, the location of your study and further ideas about sampling

- examine several possible research methods (surveys or questionnaires, interviews, observations and the use of documents)

- decide which method/s you would use for your data collection, taking into account your topic, your broad research question, the purpose of your research, your specific research question/s and the design of your study, the methods used in previous research in the area, your developing knowledge about different methods of data collection, the scale of your study and the requirements of your course or subject

• read definitions of important key terms: inter-rater reliability, member checking.

TAKING IT FURTHER

This chapter provided a starting point for learning about different methods of data collection and related issues. Once you select your methods, further reading on your chosen method/s is important. The chapters on research methods in the book listed below could help you to start to take your learning further.

FURTHER READING

Lambert, M. (2012), *A Beginner's Guide to Doing Your Education Research Project*, London: Sage.
See Chapter 7 and Chapter 8.

7
Understanding paradigms

This chapter will help you to:

 develop a basic understanding of paradigms

 identify the dominant paradigm associated with your research.

Learning about research paradigms can be very challenging at first. It can even be difficult to find definitions of the concept that are easy for novice researchers to understand, unless they have begun planning their research and have a basic knowledge about a few different paradigms as they apply to research examples.

You are in an ideal position to start thinking about research paradigms and how your research ideas align with a particular paradigm. This is because you have taken a number of opportunities to develop and refine your topic, broad research question, the purpose of your research, your specific research question/s and your ideas about a suitable research design and methods to answer your research questions, and you have taken care to ensure that all of these points are in alignment.

When the research questions, design and methods of the proposed study are aligned, informed readers/supervisors should not be surprised by students' paradigmatic positions and how they approach theory. Their intentions in regard to testing theory, building theory or contributing to existing theory, and their alignment with a particular paradigm, will be evident. Novice researchers who see these connections and have at least a basic understanding of some of the common paradigms can begin to understand the paradigmatic assumptions underlying the research reported in the evidence-based research articles in their areas of interest. They are then able to argue why they propose to take similar or different positions on approaches to theory, and how their decisions impact the overall design of their small-scale study, their sampling technique and the methods chosen for data collection. Later, they will also be able to see how their reports of their research findings reflect their paradigms.

Research and research training can begin with learning about different paradigms, or it can begin with thinking about the research questions and the purpose of the research. The first of these approaches is referred to as a **paradigmatic approach** and the second is referred to as a **pragmatic approach**. Both approaches are fine.

One reason why this book takes a pragmatic approach is because, having

Paradigmatic approach
This approach to research begins with a paradigm, which influences how the research is approached and the assumptions inherent in how the research questions are asked.

Pragmatic approach
Researchers begin with their research questions or their research problems, and select research methods that will address the research questions.

thought about what they want to find out, how they propose to find out and other possible ways of approaching their study, novice researchers have quite solid points of reference to begin learning about paradigms. By starting with basic reading, they are often in a good position to be able to identify the paradigm to which their research belongs and their own orientation to knowledge in relation to their proposed problem. The choice of reading is important at this point. Not only do readings categorise and explain paradigms differently, but the more complex readings are often easier to follow and digest after a basic level of understanding is reached.

This chapter looks at some of the key features of the research examples provided in Chapter 1 and how these studies align with particular paradigms. You may have already noticed a few key differences in the ways Louise and Maria approached their research compared with the way that I approached my research. Re-examining key features of these studies in relation to paradigms will help you to begin building knowledge about what is meant by research paradigms. You will continue to build this knowledge by identifying the paradigms used in the research reported in the articles that you chose for your literature review and then determining the paradigm to which your approach to your own research ideas belongs.

Your first opportunity to write in your notebook, however, will involve finding out how much you need to learn about paradigms to satisfy the requirements of your course or subject. As noted by Lambert (2012), it is possible to plan your first small-scale research project without knowing very much about paradigms, and this may happen to be the approach taken in your course or subject. When novice researchers have very short timeframes to plan and perhaps execute their first studies, there will be many areas where they do not have time to go far below the surface. An experienced and knowledgeable research supervisor or lecturer can guide you as to what you really need to know now and what you can explore more deeply later once you know your direction or you are undertaking more advanced studies in research methods.

My suggestion with paradigms is not to go too deeply at first, and certainly not to write more than your course or subject requires. It is better to stop writing before you get tangled and misconceptions about deeper level concepts begin to emerge. You can always build on a smaller amount of sound knowledge later. Apart from knowing your course or subject requirements in relation to paradigms, it is also important to know whether your studies commence as we did by identifying the research question or the research problem (the pragmatic approach) or whether your research training begins by thinking about your paradigm (the paradigmatic approach).

 For your notebook

Exercise 7.1 What do you need to know about paradigms for your course or subject?

Returning to your research methods course or subject outline and notes, find out whether:

- there is a section on research paradigms
- the course or subject commences with learning about paradigms (a paradigmatic approach) or with developing research questions or research problems (a pragmatic approach)
- the assignments require you to address research paradigms.

If it appears that your course or subject outline or notes do not refer to paradigms, put this exercise to one side until you work further through the chapter and learn some of the terminology and concepts associated with paradigms. Once you have this increased awareness, it would be worth looking at your course or subject outline or notes again in case you can see a connection to paradigms that perhaps was not apparent to you earlier.

PARADIGMS AND RESEARCH EXAMPLES

Here we return to the hypothetical problem about the teacher who had difficulty increasing the amounts that students wrote during creative writing lessons (Chapter 5). When considering an experimental design, we thought about comparing two methods of teaching creative writing to determine which was more effective. A research question developed for a *quasi-experiment* (given that classes rather than individuals would be assigned to methods), in addition to identifying a year level and demographics of the participating schools or classes, could ask which method was more effective—Method A or Method B—with regard to the number of words that students wrote. Here we would be *quantifying* the number of words written by each student and we would be *assuming* that we would need to be *systematic, exacting and rigorous* in our approach, and that we would arrive at an *authentic* conclusion—that is, whether the students learning under one method wrote *significantly more words* than students learning under the other method. We would test our theory by collecting quantitative data and have a scientific approach to our quasi-experiment. In Exercise 5.3, you had the opportunity to think about which experimental design you would use for this problem. The paradigm for this approach is referred to as *positivist*. A more in-depth look at this paradigm through further reading reveals that there are different types of positivism. If you are thinking about conducting quantitative research and your course or subject requires deeper knowledge about positivism, the further readings at the end of this chapter are suggested as starting points.

We took the opportunity, when looking at the key features, uses and limitations of qualitative research designs, to think about the creative writing problem in a very different way. We stripped away some of the *assumptions* that we made earlier and the idea that we had a theory to test. The focus changed to *exploring* what teachers believed to be the key reasons for the amount and quality of student work during creative writing lessons. From their ideas, we wanted to begin *building a theory* (which we could test later if we wished). We were open to ideas that would be identified and explored through the collection of *qualitative data*. Taking this approach would reflect an *interpretivist/constructivist paradigm*. It would recognise that the teachers may have different views about the problem, and that the way we thought about the problem initially may not be the only way or the only 'truth'.

Whereas positivist and interpretivist/constructivist paradigms are equally systematic, exacting and rigorous in their approach, there are times when they may not quite fit the way you think about your problem. For example, it may seem more logical to use both quantitative and qualitative methods to investigate and explore your problem or answer your research question, in which case you may find yourself using a *pragmatic paradigm*. This approach is more common now that *mixed methods* are an option for many researchers. Pragmatism gets away from the either/or situation that existed in educational research for a long time, when quantitative methods predominated and there were arguments about whether quantitative or qualitative methods were better. While this situation may not be so much of a concern now, novice researchers still need to remember that *mixed methods require a lot more knowledge and skill on the part of the researcher.* To some extent, whether this will be a problem depends on the complexity of the quantitative data collection and analysis—especially for students who do not have a statistics background. A related consideration is whether quantitative or qualitative methods predominate, or the degree of emphasis placed on each relative to the other. If you are thinking about pragmatism and you wish to argue for collecting both quantitative and qualitative data, then it is worth having conversations with your research supervisor or lecturer about the particular *type of data* you think that you need to collect, the *order* in which you propose to collect quantitative and qualitative data, the *relative emphasis* that you might give to each and *how they complement one another* in your study. While in general it could be said that novice researchers are often advised to use either quantitative or qualitative methods, in some situations it is a good idea to use both. You might like to think about the creative writing problem and how the number of words that students write during creative writing lessons could be the catalyst for exploring teachers' views.

One other paradigm that is sometimes relevant is the *transformative paradigm*, discussed by McMillan and Schumacher (2010). Investigating problems that are based on gender, race, culture or social issues often adds other layers of complexity for novice researchers conducting their first studies. As you can probably see from the areas discussed in each chapter so far (and that does not include thinking about how to analyse data, which is a focus of Chapter 8) there is a lot of learning associated with planning and conducting your first small-scale study. Even so, you may be interested to read further about this paradigm. It is feasible, for example, that an experienced researcher who identified deep-rooted gender or cultural issues affecting student performances in creative writing lessons or the way that the lessons were constructed in certain contexts might lean towards a transformative paradigm. Novice researchers planning their first, small-scale studies, however, are more likely to find that their research fits into one of the other paradigms.

Looking closely at the distinguishing features of these four paradigms reveals that the differences go deeper than the type of data they generate. They each make different assumptions about the nature of knowledge and how we understand the world. We discovered this by working through different ways of looking at the creative writing problem. We could have adopted our first idea of testing the theory that one method of teaching could be more effective than another for increasing the number of words that students write during creative writing lessons. Had we stayed with the positivist paradigm and not persisted in thinking about the problem in different ways, we would not have discovered that another theoretical framework or paradigm could have illuminated our understanding even further.

The approaches to thinking about problems in education have shifted over the years, such that we are not so constricted now by a single, dominant view or paradigm. The next exercise for your notebook provides you with the opportunity to revisit the research examples from Chapter 1 and consider different ways in which the problems could have been investigated.

For your notebook

Exercise 7.2 Other ways that research could be conducted using a different paradigm

Consider other ways in which one of the research studies (provided as examples in Chapter 1) could have been conducted.

- Perhaps Louise could have *measured* the extent to which the parents in her program were satisfied with the content and delivery of the program.

- Perhaps I could have added another part to my study and *explored* through semi-structured interviews pre-service teachers' thoughts about factors that they thought could impact on how confident they were to solve problems in mathematics.

- Perhaps I could have explored through semi-structured interviews pre-service teachers' thoughts about factors that impacted on how confident they were to teach others to solve problems in mathematics.

How would these ideas or your suggestions alter the research paradigm?

We have seen from our discussion that different ways of viewing the original, hypothetical problem of students not being very productive during their creative writing lessons open up a diversity of perspectives. The value of taking the time to think about problems in different ways shows us a range of possibilities about the nature of the problem and helps us to avoid another problem: that of being too hasty in conceptualising the problem or in deciding on the particular focus for our research.

One reason why novice researchers may find it difficult

to read about research paradigms is that readings about paradigms often categorise paradigms differently. For example, some writers refer to quantitative and qualitative paradigms, while others use categories such as positivist, interpretivist/ constructivist (either separately or as a singular approach), pragmatist and transformative. While it could be a little less confusing if all writers used the same terminology, that is not something that we can resolve and it is not likely to happen.

Deeper insights can perhaps be gained by thinking about the differences between quantitative and qualitative approaches as more than simply referring to whether data are in the form of numbers (quantitative) or in the form of words (qualitative). Combining this basic comparison with the earlier discussion about particular paradigms can help us to appreciate how research that involves data in the form or numbers and/or data in the form of words could be seen as paradigms. When choosing to collect data in the form of numbers, for example, researchers make *assumptions* about what knowledge in their particular area is like. It is assumed that if it is appropriate to conceive of the knowledge numerically, researchers need to be *systematic* in their collection and treatment of numerical data and that the approach is *exacting and rigorous*, pointing to research designs such as experiments, quasi-experiments, single-subject or correlational designs. It is also assumed that it is appropriate to *test theories* rather than to explore perceptions and build theories—especially where inferential statistics are involved. When writers refer to quantitative and qualitative paradigms, therefore, they are thinking more deeply than whether the data are quantitative or qualitative.

When research questions incorporate words that indicate the type of data to be collected, and the choice of research design and methods are all in alignment with each other, there will also be alignment to particular paradigms. An article written by Mackenzie and Knipe (2006), listed in the Further Reading section at the end of this chapter, is well worth reading. These writers summarised on a table and discussed in the surrounding text the connections between paradigms and the particular research designs and methods associated with each paradigm. Again, you will find some differences between the terms used by Mackenzie and Knipe and some other authors, but it is possible to see beyond those differences to the points being made. My suggestion is to read the entire article first so that the table that summarises the connections between paradigms, research designs and methods and the surrounding text can be understood more deeply.

IDENTIFYING PARADIGMS IN RESEARCH REPORTS

Research that is reported as articles in journals is often limited by word counts. While there is some variation between journals regarding the required minimum and maximum lengths of articles, with quantitative research reports often having fewer words, there is not always the space to talk at length about the paradigm to which the research belongs. Sometimes, for example, authors may simply note in the abstract that the research was qualitative. You may need to read the abstract, methods and results or findings sections of the report carefully for hints about the paradigm; at other times, though, the authors may be more explicit. The starting point for the reader in many cases may be in first determining whether the research used quantitative, qualitative or mixed methods. To confirm your developing thoughts, you then need to read more deeply.

The next exercise for your notebook provides you with the opportunity to look again at the articles that you used in your literature review (or identified for future writing of your literature review) in a different way. Just as you would expect to see alignment between the problem and the research questions through to the design and methods chosen for the study, all these points are also expected to be consistent with the research paradigm that is either explicitly stated or implicit in the reading of the article. For example, where the problem, research questions, design and methods all point to testing a theory using quantitative methods and statistics, you would anticipate a form of positivism. Where researchers explore problems from the perspectives of individuals who may have different perceptions or perceptions that are socially constructed, you might expect an interpretivist or constructivist paradigm. Mixed methods may point towards a pragmatic paradigm, particularly if one method does not dominate the other. Understanding the paradigms used in previous research in your area helps you to situate your own research and to know and perhaps argue why your research needs to continue in the same tradition or to use a different paradigm.

 For your notebook

Exercise 7.3 What paradigms were used in the research that you included in your literature review?

Return to the research articles used in your literature review or identified for inclusion in a literature review to determine which paradigm was used in each reported research project.

Check whether there is any specific reference to paradigms in each article and also look for evidence that either is consistent with the paradigm taken or use this evidence to identify the paradigm if it is not identified specifically by the author(s).

Copy the table that you created for Exercise 4.4 and add an extra row just above the comments row on your table. The extra row is for the paradigm. Also add to the comments row notes about how you determined the paradigm of each study from the reading of its research article.

Write a short paragraph summarising the paradigms used in the reports of previous research in your area.

WHICH PARADIGM WILL YOU USE?

Now think about your approach to your proposed study in the context of previous research by completing the following exercise in your notebook.

 For your notebook

Exercise 7.4 To which research paradigm does your research belong?

Take your own topic, broad research question, purpose statement, specific research question(s) and your chosen research design and methods:

- Identify the paradigm to which your research belongs.

- Explain how the above details about your research are consistent with this paradigm and not consistent with other research paradigms.

- Drawing on your response to Exercise 7.3, comment briefly on how your choice of paradigm is the same as, different from or complements the paradigms used in previous studies in your area.

DEFINING THE CONCEPT OF THE PARADIGM

Now that you have some knowledge about the main research paradigms, it is probably reasonably easy for you to construct a definition of each of these paradigms.

Perhaps more elusive is the art of defining paradigms more generally—especially providing definitions that are lucid and easy to understand by novice researchers. You may wish to find and read some definitions provided in research methods literature before or after completing the next exercise. Sometimes it is easier to think clearly and more creatively by constructing your own definition first.

 For your notebook

Exercise 7.5 Defining the concept of the paradigm

Based on your developing knowledge of paradigms and drawing on the discussion and related notebook exercises completed in this chapter, provide a simple and clear definition of 'paradigm' that you think would be understood by novice researchers.

 For your notebook

Exercise 7.6 Proposing a definition of paradigms

Consult with a few other novice researchers who have also been working on a definition of paradigm.

- Together look at the proposed definitions, make refinements as necessary and jointly propose one or more definitions that could be understood by other novice researchers.

> • Now show the definitions to other novice researchers (perhaps some who have not heard about paradigms). Do they understand the definitions?

CONCLUDING THOUGHTS

My advice to novice researchers is not to worry if some readings about paradigms seem too complex and confusing at first. Other readings can be put in their place, with the option of returning to the more difficult readings later if there is a need to deepen and expand knowledge. A few well-chosen readings on paradigms once the research questions are drafted and choices about research designs and methods are made can make the learning simpler. It is paramount in the early stages to be aware of the requirements of your course or subject, and it may not be necessary to go too deeply into paradigms in the early stages of research training. Sometimes it is possible to avoid getting 'tangled up' in your writing if you know when to stop!

At this early stage, if you can see a neat alignment between your research questions, design and methods and one of the paradigms explained in this chapter, then that could be sufficient for you—or perhaps provide you with enough of an introduction to the area to be able to explore paradigms further with other reading.

Just as research training can begin with discussions around paradigms or commence by asking students to think about a topic, construct draft research questions and then following through with planning a small-scale study in that area before considering paradigms, experienced researchers can also approach their research from either direction. My personal preference is to start with the research question or problem but my knowledge of paradigms means that I am simultaneously aware of the paradigmatic positioning of my research questions, depending on the way that I phrase my questions.

If you were to go back to the beginning of this book after working through this chapter and to plan the same or another small-scale study, it is also likely that, even though you would again foreground your research questions (referred to as a pragmatic rather than a paradigmatic approach), you might concurrently be cognisant of your paradigmatic position. You could also feel that further selected reading around paradigms would be easier to understand due to having that background, compared to not having your own research ideas and some knowledge around research designs and methods first. Having your own ideas first provides a good reference point for learning about paradigms.

CHAPTER SUMMARY

In this chapter, you took the time to:

- check whether the requirements of your course or subject include learning about paradigms and whether your course or subject begins with research questions and research problems or with learning about paradigms

- examine the research examples from Chapter 1 again to determine to which paradigms they belong and how we know

- look again at the articles that you used for or set aside for a literature review to determine to which paradigms those studies belong

- revisit your ideas for your own small-scale research project to determine the paradigm to which your research belongs

- develop a definition of research paradigms that is easy for novice researchers without any knowledge of paradigms to understand

- read definitions of paradigmatic approach and pragmatic approach.

FURTHER READING

Mackenzie, N. & Knipe, S. (2006), Research Dilemmas: Paradigms, methods and methodology, *Issues in Educational Research*, *16*(2), pp. 193–205.

Read the whole article and then go back to Table 2, which provides a concise overview of different paradigms and which research methods are suitable for each.

Punch, K.F. (2014), *Introduction to Research Methods in Education* (2nd ed.), London: Sage.

See pp. 18–21 on paradigms.

8
Data analysis

This chapter will help you to:

 understand the concepts underpinning the analysis of qualitative and quantitative data from surveys or questionnaires, interviews and observations

 work towards the analysis of qualitative and/or quantitative data for your small-scale study.

The first time that you work through this chapter will be during the planning stage of your small-scale study and before you start your data collection. This is because you need to plan in advance how your research problem and questions, the design of your study, your sample size and sampling method, and your methods of data collection and analysis align. Rechecking the alignment between the earlier parts when planning your data analysis enables you to do a final check that all of the preceding parts are likely to work as well as you anticipated and that plans for data analysis confirm the underlying logic of your study.

If you plan to collect both qualitative and quantitative data, an early reading of this chapter and finding out what assistance you can access for learning about data entry and analysis as appropriate for both approaches gives you the opportunity to think about whether using mixed methods is a realistic option for you. On reflection, you may decide that using a single approach will make your task more manageable and be possible within your given timeframe. In other words, the iterative process of toggling back and forth between the research questions and the other parts of your plan continues throughout this chapter and, if you are in the planning stages of your work, there is still time to make further adjustments to your plan if necessary.

On first engagement with this chapter, you might also identify additional readings related to areas that are important for your particular research, which you explore deeply to complement your learning. The further readings listed at the end of this chapter are suggested starting points.

Thinking ahead of time about *how* you will analyse your data before you commence your data collection is also important if you are required to document these plans in advance, perhaps as part of your research proposal. You may even take classes or training in how to use computer programs to enter and analyse or assist with the analysis of data. If your data are quantitative, some statistical training or guidance is likely to be required. There are also computer programs that can assist you to analyse qualitative data, although whether you need to use one of these programs if you have a small data set, can be decided with your research supervisor or lecturer.

Later reading of this chapter, particularly the parts that align with your quantitative, qualitative or mixed-methods approach to your study, is likely to be undertaken when you are ready to enter or prepare your data for analysis. Where possible, entering data can be an ongoing process as the data become available. This is often the case with qualitative research, in which case data analysis commonly commences during data collection. When all the data are collected simultaneously, which is often the case with quantitative research data, input and analysis begin immediately after the data are collected.

This chapter is organised around the methods of data collection (surveys/questionnaires, interviews and observations) that were the main focus of Chapter 6. The focus is initially on working towards the analysis of qualitative data for each of these methods, followed by the analysis of quantitative data for the same methods. The conclusion presents some further points to consider if you decide that your research could involve the collection and analysis of qualitative and quantitative data.

WORKING TOWARDS ANALYSING QUALITATIVE DATA

My best advice for novice researchers using qualitative methods is to keep the research as simple and straightforward as possible. Even so—and almost inevitably—research is more complex than we anticipate. Experienced researchers can be more adventurous. They will often have broader research questions, but they also have the skills to analyse qualitative data for which themes are not always predetermined.

The danger for novice researchers with a broader approach is that they can end up with a lot of data and little obvious or clear direction about what they are looking for at the outset. This could present difficulties—for example, when conducting interviews, which are then likely to have little structure.

They may spend a lot of time trying to work out where to start with the data analysis and could feel overwhelmed and worried about meeting the deadline for the submission of their research report.

The general advice often given to novice researchers nowadays is to have quite specific research questions to guide their studies. The methods that they use to collect data, such as qualitative surveys or questionnaires, semi-structured interviews and/or qualitative observations, are designed to address specific research questions, but they can still leave the way open for participants in the research to present their perspectives. For example, Louise had two research questions: one relating to what participants thought about the content of the program for young and prospective young parents and one relating to the delivery of the program. The questions that she asked in her qualitative survey and in the focus group interview explored these two areas. It is not so difficult, then, to decide which data relate to which research question, although it can also be possible that some responses relate to both research questions—perhaps because of connections between them. Even so, focus groups can still provide room for deeper explanations and even unanticipated points to be raised by participants. This was particularly important in Louise's research because she carried the dual role of the author of the program that was being evaluated and the researcher. She needed to take care that her views as the author of the program did not cloud her thinking as a researcher.

Determining how the data will be analysed under the research questions is another step to consider before the data are collected. That is an ideal time to:

- read about different approaches to analysing qualitative data
- examine how other researchers analysed their data, and
- work towards choosing an approach to data analysis that is as simple as possible and meaningful for you.

As McMillan and Schumacher (2010) note, there can be some variation in the ways individual researchers approach the analysis of their qualitative data, although the possibilities are not completely open. Particularly in your first study, qualitative data analysis can be a journey of discovery, as you find out what works best for you and for your data. This means that some of your initial thoughts about how you could analyse your data may change as you start working with your data.

A little later in this chapter you will examine one way of analysing qualitative data. This 'hands-on' approach or something similar could be a good way for you to do your data analysis, especially as your small data set provides the ideal opportunity to get close to your data and make some discoveries about the nature of qualitative data and data analysis. I often advise novice researchers to take a hands-on approach to their qualitative data analysis, at least when conducting their first study. You could, however, consider using a computer program such as NVivo to assist with this process. NVivo is one of the more commonly used programs and is likely to be available at your university. It is important for you to check your subject requirements first, however, as you may be required to go one way or the other or you may have a choice.

Some fundamental points

Qualitative research:

- involves the collection of *data in the form of words*, such as responses to questions on qualitative surveys or in interviews, or field notes taken by the researcher while observing teachers in action
- generally places emphasis on *building theory* (and working *inductively* with the data) in preference to testing theory (working deductively with the data) in order to identify and explore themes related to the research question/s
- may have *less-specific research questions* than quantitative research, although novice researchers are advised not to have research questions that are too broad
- may entail *exploring* the perceptions or ideas of one or more participants
- may involve *more than one data collection method*
- often provides the opportunity for data analysis to begin *as the data are being collected*, especially when the data are collected progressively—for example, from one participant then another, or from one method of data collection followed by another with the same participants, or with a sub-set of the original participants for the second method of data collection
- is an *iterative process* whereby data in the form of words are examined as they become available, with the researcher moving back and forth between earlier and later data, progressively analysing and interpreting the data to find answers to the research questions
- can lead to *challenges in managing and analysing large data sets* (for example, if using one or more broad research questions, a narrative research design and

unstructured interviews with multiple participants). This is why novice researchers are encouraged to think *small scale*. The *timeframe* for completing the research, from the initial planning to the presentation of the research report, is also a consideration.

Despite the advice to novice researchers to develop quite specific research questions, there are times when a broader approach is more appropriate. For example, some areas of interest to educational researchers are quite new, so broader research questions are needed in the initial stages of the study to enable the researcher to work towards generating a theory to explain the phenomenon. When not so much is known about an area and researchers feel that they cannot be as specific as they intend to be with their first, small-scale study, they need to be more open-minded about what they might find. As they find out more, researchers might then be able to ask more specific questions—either to explore the developing theory further or even to begin to test the theory and do some deductive work.

These are some of the key features of an approach known as *grounded theory*, which developed through the work of Glaser and Strauss (see Punch and Oancea, 2014). You may be interested in pursuing reading about grounded theory later, but for the present you will begin to develop many skills around planning, conducting and reporting a small-scale study that could be a good foundation for later moving into more complex areas of research.

My suggestion for novice researchers planning or undertaking their first small-scale study and with a limited timeframe is to take a less-sophisticated approach. Even after spending considerable time doing the extra reading and learning while putting your developing research ideas on hold, you may still decide that grounded theory is not for you.

Perhaps, instead, you can see some synergies with Louise's situation. She also had a tight timeframe in which to complete a literature review, plan her study, develop her research proposal, gain ethical clearance to collect her data, administer her qualitative survey and conduct semi-structured interviews, analyse her data and write her research report. Later, Louise and I worked together so that Louise could begin to learn about the process of writing for possible publication and the findings from her research could be disseminated. If appropriate, you might also look for these types of opportunities.

LOUISE'S RESEARCH: KEY POINTS

As a reminder, here are key points about Louise's small-scale, qualitative study presented as Example 1 in Chapter 1.

Student project: Evaluation of a program

Louise Wightman, a student who worked at a community centre, designed an education program to support young parents or young prospective parents in the early stages of parenthood. Louise delivered parts of the program and arranged for other professionals to deliver the remaining parts of the program. She was keen to find out from the participants in the program what they thought about both the content of the program and how it was delivered so that strengths and ways to enhance the program could be identified. Her research therefore evaluated the content and delivery of the program from the perspectives of the participants.

- Louise's broad *topic* was community education programs for young parents and young prospective parents.

- The *problem* that interested Louise was a practical one related to making decisions about the content and delivery of education programs to meet the needs of young and prospective young parents.
- A *broad research question* around the above scenario could be: 'What do young parents and prospective young parents look for in community education programs designed to help them adjust to parenthood?'
- While this was posed as a possible broad research question, Louise's actual broad research question was: 'What does lifelong learning mean in the context of the lives of women who become mothers as teenagers?'
- This broad research question linked back to *lifelong learning theory*.
- The *purpose* of Louise's research was to identify from the perspectives of participants in an education program for young parents strengths and areas for further enhancement in the content and delivery of the program that she had designed.
- This was a *small-scale study* conducted by an education student who had never previously conducted research. It shows how an interest in the education of a particular group can be the catalyst for a number of possible small-scale research projects of a size that is manageable for a single novice researcher.

Louise situated her work within lifelong learning (Wightman & Moriarty, 2012), but her two specific research questions were:

- How effective was the content of the Young Parents Program in meeting the needs of participants?

- How effective did the participants in the Young Parents Program find the delivery of the program?

As explained by Wightman and Moriarty (2012), Louise's qualitative survey provided background, biographical and behavioural information from the eight participants in her research that could then be explored more deeply with the four participants who also took part in the focus group interview. Key to Louise's success in answering her specific research questions was the way her sample was chosen, particularly in ensuring that the participants represented the diversity of life circumstances found among the fifteen women who completed the program across the year, and that those who took part in the focus group interview were selected on the basis of the range of responses provided on the qualitative survey. This approach to the selection of a smaller *sample* of participants for the focus group interview illustrates how the analysis of data collected earlier in a qualitative study can *impact further data collection.*

The attention given to selecting the participants, particularly for the focus group interview, facilitated the data analysis and also helped to ensure that Louise was able to foreground participants' (rather than her own) perspectives of the program, as it would be easy to introduce an element of bias when the researcher was also the author of the program. To be as truly representative of the range of views of the total number of mothers who completed the program, it was important for the diversity of views to be tapped into during the data collection, thus providing the opportunity for the same to occur with the data analysis. These points are important because they illustrate the close *connections between data collection and data analysis.*

You should now locate the Wightman and Moriarty (2012) article listed in the Further Reading section at the end of this chapter. Examining reports of research is also helpful to gain some ideas about how you can write these parts of your own research report. This point will be expanded in Chapter 10. Articles are much more restricted in the maximum word limits allowable compared with theses, and sometimes even compared with shorter research reports that novice researchers complete as regular assignments. Even so, reading this report of Louise's research will help to illustrate a few important points relating to the underlying logic that existed between Louise's research questions, conceptual framework, data collection and analysis and the presentation of the results and findings.

 For your notebook

Exercise 8.1 Louise's methods section of a report of her research

The *methods* section of the article that reported Louise's research provides a snapshot of how the research was conducted, how the data were analysed and key information needed before reading the *results* section of the article. Read the methods section of the article and take notes on the following points:

- the *purpose* of the research (both in broader and more specific terms): why the research was important and to whom

- the *participants*: how they were *selected* from among the women who undertook the young parents program and how *representation* was achieved (albeit that the sample was also one of convenience)

• *data-collection methods* (including reasons for choosing the methods) and brief reference to *how the data were analysed* (including *inductive analysis* and *coding of emerging concepts and themes*) and practical information on how a table was constructed to facilitate the data analysis

Label your response 'Exercise 8.1 Louise's methods section of a report of her research'.

This understanding now provides an ideal background for looking more closely at the methods used for analysing the data (as proposed in the methods section of the article). Key words include *inductive analysis* and *coding of emerging concepts and themes*.

Also worth considering further is the idea of selecting participants, such that the sample represents as far as possible the variety of participants in the program and their circumstances.

Analysing qualitative data

Louise used a process called *inductive analysis*, drawn from McMillan and Schumacher (2006) and also explained by McMillan and Schumacher (2010). Examining how Louise applied inductive analysis to her project may help you to think about whether this approach would be useful and appropriate for you. The results section of the publication that came from Louise's work provides some explanation in the methods section about how she undertook her data analysis.

Typically, researchers do not provide very detailed information in their articles about how they approached their data analysis because they are restricted by word count. Theses, however, have more space for the data analysis techniques used to be explained. Even some assignments could provide that opportunity.

Working from Louise's explanation of how she approached her data analysis, we will now 'look behind the scenes' to see how qualitative data analysis can occur.

Louise took an approach to her data analysis that is often recommended to novice researchers. Many established researchers also take this approach. Louise's data analysis and the report of her results and findings were guided by her two specific research questions.

The following technique explains practical ways of proceeding from the raw data to the point of having identified themes that fall under each research question. This approach logically leads to the same structure being used for the presentation of the findings, as you will see later in Louise's research report, where she discusses themes that she identified under each research question. We will focus on interview data here, but a similar procedure could be followed for the analysis of qualitative data from surveys.

After having completed the transcripts of the interviews that you conducted, you could do the following:

- Print the transcripts using one side of the paper only. If you have a very small number of interview transcripts, each could be printed on different coloured paper if you prefer. Use fairly wide margins to allow for notes to be written later. Include the questions asked as well as the answers under each question. Include the research question in bold at the top if you had just one. Include the second question further down as appropriate, also in bold.
- Read through the first transcript to get a feel for what

is there and to jog your memory of the interview. Perhaps read another transcript.

- Return to the first transcript, and identify and mark out individual sections that form logical blocks or segments—for example, around similar points in the discussion. Some of these blocks of words or segments will be quite short, while others will be longer. You might simply put a vertical line in the margin to indicate where individual segments said by the participant as well as the researcher start and finish. Read through again and check your work. If your research was conducted in a team—for example, with a class member—it is recommended that you do this task individually at first and then discuss and compare your work. Following this discussion, you may decide to make adjustments to where you noted the start and finish of some segments.

- Go back to each segment of words one at a time and write a single word or just a few words that describe the segment. These words are called *codes*. As you proceed down the page, keep toggling back to earlier codes to compare their content and the label that you have given them so that you start to see where codes are repeated. This is where using one side of the paper only enables you to spread the pages across your desk for ease of comparison. Longer segments may even have several codes. If so, clearly show where these occur within the segment—for example, by underlining the words and having the code in the margin beside the underlined words. Again, if you are working with a colleague, do this individually at first and then compare and discuss the decisions that you made.

- Take out your next interview transcript and go through

the same procedure, repeating all the above steps. If you are working with a colleague, work separately again at first. This approach makes the most of your individual and combined wisdom. While you are looking at this next set of data, you are constantly testing whether the code descriptions that you identified from reading the first transcript still fit. This is a point for further reflection (and discussion if you are working with a colleague, particularly if you came up with slightly different ideas), and can lead to some adjustments being made to your codes.

- Be more creative and work to your preferences. The aim of this step is to group similar codes together to form logical categories or themes. This can be done with the paper copies of the transcripts using different coloured felt pens for each category. It can also involve transferring the information onto tables, and this could also mean copying across the quotes from participants for each code and theme. It can even be helpful to do the colour coding on the paper first before working on the tables electronically. As you do this work, you will decide on the approach that suits you best, which may be a variation on the suggestions proposed here.

Louise briefly described her approach to the data analysis at the end of the methods section of the article and then used the first paragraph of the results section to introduce the themes that emerged under each research question. She then discussed the themes under each heading separately, drawing on participants' words to illuminate the themes.

Even if you have just one or two interview transcripts, it is not possible or expected that you will use all of the words provided by the participants when discussing the findings under the themes in the report. Just as you considered carefully how you would select your participants for your study, you will think carefully about which passages from the interview data to include in the results or findings sections of your report. It is important to be true to the meaning intended by participants and their range of views, and to show how you interpreted their words. This transparency is important as readers were not present during the interviews and are not privy to the full transcripts. This is an ethical consideration and quite a responsibility, as you are the conduit between the participants and readers of your research report.

The following exercise will help you to analyse the broad structure of the results section of Louise's research report. Even though your topic is likely to be different from Louise's, it is still worthwhile looking at how other researchers structure their reports.

 For your notebook

Exercise 8.2 Louise's results section of her research report

The results section of the article (Wightman & Moriarty, 2012) begins with a paragraph indicating that the analysis of the data from the qualitative surveys and the focus group interviews together revealed five main themes emerging in relation to each of the two research questions. The results are then presented separately under each research question.

- Read the paragraph directly under the heading *Results* and draw a diagram, with labels, that lists the *themes* that emerged under each research question.

- Using a printout of the results section, highlight where each theme is introduced under each research question.

- Note the variations as well as similarities in responses given by participants. These comparisons and distinctions were possible only because the participants were selected based on the range of circumstances represented by the women who undertook the program. The selection of the sample was therefore very important.

Label your response 'Exercise 8.2 Louise's results section of her research report'.

You have effectively recreated from the presentation of the results the information that Louise inductively drew from the data as described in the last paragraph of the *methods* section of the report. In that paragraph, Louise briefly explained how she constructed a table so that she could record the concepts and themes as they emerged from her inductive analysis of the data related to each research question.

We know that there is no single, universal approach taken by researchers when analysing qualitative data. You will need to decide on an approach that suits you and the data that you collect. Exercise 8.3 will facilitate your examination of how other researchers described their approaches to the analysis of their qualitative data.

 For your notebook

Exercise 8.3 What approaches to data analysis were used in qualitative evidence-based research articles in your area of interest?

- Return to your list of evidence-based research articles that you used in your literature review or identified for future writing of your literature review.

- Scan the articles and your notes for each article and place the articles into three groups as appropriate. The groups consist of articles that report research that used:
  - qualitative methods only
  - quantitative methods only (note the statistical tables used in the results sections)
  - mixed methods.

- Leave aside for the next parts of this chapter the articles that reported quantitative research and mixed methods (combining quantitative and qualitative research).

- Working with the evidence-based articles that reported *qualitative research* in your *area of interest*, draw up and complete a table that summarises these reports and the approaches taken to analyse the qualitative data.

Area	Article 1 (author/year)	Article 2 (author/year)	Article 3 (author/year)
Abstract			
Key themes/main authors referenced			
Definitions/debates			
Research question/s			
Methods, including descriptions of how the data were analysed			
Results or findings			
Implications			
Comments			

- If you completed Exercise 4.4 in your notebook, you will have most of the above information already, and will just need to add *descriptions of how the qualitative*

- *data were analysed* (if found in the methods section) and particularly *check the results or findings sections*. Note for each article whether there is a results section and a findings section or just one or the other.

- For several of these articles, draw diagrams with labels, which list or summarise the themes that emerged (under each research question if appropriate) and depict the processes used to analyse the qualitative data.

- Note any references to research methods literature relating to the analysis of qualitative data that were used in the methods sections of these articles. You may find the references to research methods literature (or updated versions) useful starting points for your further reading. The full bibliographic details are in the references at the end of the article. Locate these references for later use in Taking It Further towards the end of this chapter.

Label your response 'Exercise 8:3 What approaches to data analysis were used in qualitative evidence-based research articles in your area of interest?'

WORKING TOWARDS ANALYSING QUANTITATIVE DATA

A number of steps are involved in working with quantitative data collected from surveys or questionnaires, structured interviews or structured observations:

- choosing the appropriate *statistical tests*
- choosing an appropriate *statistical package* (unless you are doing your calculations by hand). One of the most commonly used packages available for Mac or PC is SPSS (Statistical Product and Service Solutions, formerly Statistical Package for the Social Sciences)
- *entering the data* onto an appropriate spreadsheet

- undertaking the *data analysis* or doing the calculations, and then
- *interpreting and presenting the results* in relation to your research questions.

Following on from these points, Chapter 9 helps you to think about the *findings and implications* for future practice and research, while Chapter 10 focuses on presenting your research report.

Before collecting your data, you can experiment with entering (hypothetical) data into a spreadsheet using a *statistical package* such as SPSS and trial-run a few calculations. You can also work through tutorials available in the program. Of course, you need to be sure that you *understand which statistical tests are appropriate*, taking into account limitations imposed by the size of your sample for your small-scale study and by the particular sampling method used. Many novice researchers will use small convenience samples, although some may use larger samples—for example, if they employ quantitative surveys as their only method of data collection.

In one respect, it does not really matter whether you have a statistical background before you start planning your small-scale quantitative research project. It could be argued that the important point is to develop the necessary understanding relevant to your project by the time you submit your research report. On the other hand, it is also important to consider your timeframe and available resources. If the timeframe is short and you do not have a mentor who can work with you to explain what you need to know and guide you at each stage of the process, then a quantitative study may only be a realistic option for those with at least some statistical background knowledge. You might also be guided by your level of comfort when reading about quantitative designs in Chapter 5, quantitative methods in Chapter 6 and the section on working towards the analysis of quantitative data in this chapter.

As with choosing your research design and methods, a philosophical approach in which you learn *why it is appropriate to use a particular statistical test* and not others, and to recognise the *limitations of your project* that guide your decisions, is powerful. Someone with this broader and more in-depth knowledge, who understands the **underlying assumptions** that need to be met before certain statistical tests can be used, is better placed to guide you than another student or family member who perhaps knows just a little about statistics.

Statistics is one of those areas where a little knowledge can be dangerous. Making connections early in the planning stages of your project with people who are not just a few steps ahead of you is important, and can help to make the process more successful, enjoyable and rewarding. It would be a pity to plan your project and collect your data before realising that you would have made one or two different decisions if you had taken this advice ahead of time.

Underlying assumptions
While some statistical tests may appear to be obvious choices to answer the research question, some—such as correlations—require certain assumptions to be met regarding the data in order for it to be appropriate to use the test. These assumptions are tested with the data first. If the assumptions are met, then the proposed tests can be conducted.

At a higher level of study, you would be expected to have more knowledge and a deeper understanding of statistics, but we need to remember that this is your first quantitative project and you are just beginning to learn the process. We also need to remember that your first small-scale project will not produce ground-breaking findings or discoveries.

Instead, it is an opportunity for you to begin to learn how to be systematic in investigating issues that challenge you or make you curious in your current or future professional life.

Once you are reassured that all the parts of your plan for your small-scale study are in alignment and the statistical tests that you need to use have been determined, it is time to think about *how you will enter your data into a spreadsheet, analyse your data* and *interpret and present the results* according to your research questions. There are many step-by-step guides available, showing how to open SPSS and enter data, but it is also worthwhile sitting down with someone when you begin the process. It is also highly beneficial to ask about introductory workshops—especially workshops that enable you to focus on your own research, data entry and data analysis. Finding out about possible workshops or individual help well ahead of time is advisable so that you can take advantage of any available opportunities offered within your timeframe. You will find that, once everything is in place, you will do the analysis quite quickly, leaving you more time to write the results section of your research report.

Given your short timeframe and the availability of SPSS for Mac and PC (as well as the tutorials they provide), you could be shown the 'short-cut' method of undertaking the analysis. This involves using menus and drop-down boxes rather than the more in-depth approach of designing a **code book** in which you write the instructions (**syntax**) that the program will use to achieve the same ends. If you continue your studies to a higher level later, you may find that you learn more advanced procedures than you need for your first small-scale project. For your first study,

Code book A collection of instructions (syntax) for analysing data in SPSS.

Syntax The instructions designed for analysis of data entered into SPSS.

however, a good guide or mentor will help to make the process much simpler than it sounds!

It is now time to pause and inquire about assistance that you may be able to access and any relevant introductory workshops, podcasts or online training to work with quantitative data that are available to you.

 For your notebook

Exercise 8.4 What assistance in statistics is available to you?

Consult your course notes and then your research supervisor or lecturer to clarify whether you can access basic and appropriate online training, podcasts or workshops in statistics, and data entry and analysis, particularly where you can use your own data as part of the training.

Can your research supervisor or lecturer provide help or is there someone else who can provide assistance on an individual basis?

Label your response 'Exercise 8.4 What assistance in statistics is available to you?'

Talking with someone who has a lot of statistical knowledge and expertise is important. You will need to provide such a person with the following information and be prepared to clarify any points:

- the *purpose of your study* and your *research questions*
- how your choice of *research design* (for example, a particular quasi-experiment or a correlational design) fits with your research questions

- how you designed or selected your *data-collection instrument/s* in line with your *conceptual framework* to address your research questions
- your *sample size* and *how you selected* or intend to select your sample
- a copy of your (draft) *data-collection instrument/s* (such as a quantitative survey, a structured interview schedule, a structured observation schedule or an achievement test).

Even if you have a strong statistical background and can determine which statistical tests are relevant for your research, a good guide will still want to discuss the above points to confirm that you are on the right track. Only then is it appropriate to receive help in selecting the appropriate statistical tests and getting started with your data entry and analysis and later, interpreting and presenting the results.

Particularly fundamental among these points is not just your *sample size* but *how you selected your sample*. For example, your method of sampling has implications for whether your sample is regarded as being representative of the *population* from which it came, so you can be fairly confident that equivalent results would be obtained from another sample from the same population. In other words, under the right conditions you are able not only to *describe* and later *discuss* the results that came from your sample (using *descriptive statistics*), but also to make *inferences* based on these results to the population to which your sample belongs.

This is possibly the most difficult condition to meet in a first, small-scale study that is planned, conducted and reported within a short timeframe. Many such samples will be convenience samples that do not have the same hallmarks of random samples. If this is a *limitation* in your study, then it will need to be recognised in your research report because it has implications for how the findings of your study can be applied. While limitations such as this one may not be acceptable at a higher level of study, it is often the case that they can be cautiously noted and accepted at this level. All studies have their limitations.

FUNDAMENTAL CONCEPTS TO UNDERSTAND

When undertaking your first quantitative study, it is helpful to make yourself familiar with a number of fundamental concepts. *Do not be too concerned about trying to keep all of these concepts and what they mean in your head or if some concepts seem a little deep.* If your small-scale study is quantitative, you can always look back and, as you relate them to your own study and begin to use the terminology in your discussions, it is likely that they will mean more to you.

Fundamental concepts to understand include:

- substantive and statistical research questions and answers
- types of variables
- levels of measurement (nominal, ordinal, interval and ratio)
- descriptive and inferential statistics
- statistical significance, probability and p-values
- normal distribution.

This is not an exhaustive list, but it is a good start.

It would be helpful to have a little understanding about these concepts before you visit your research supervisor, lecturer or adviser to determine which statistical tests are appropriate for your research. Even some basic awareness of the terminology or ideas before you get too deep with your discussions could mean that you gain some familiarity, which will ensure that the process and language are not quite so strange. There are many other concepts that you would eventually aim to understand as well, although building such knowledge and understanding takes considerable time. Again, this is your first opportunity to plan, conduct and report a small-scale study, so you should not be too concerned that there will be some areas where you will need to show 'trust' in your adviser. This does not mean devolving all responsibility, but simply being reasonable about what you should expect to achieve as a novice researcher.

Substantive and statistical research questions and answers

The *research questions* that you developed earlier in your planning are regarded as *substantive questions* because they relate to *theory* and to your *conceptual framework*, even though the wording may indicate whether you will use quantitative, qualitative or mixed methods. The person guiding you through your quantitative study may ask you to develop *statistical questions* that relate to your original (substantive) questions or work with you through this process so that the appropriate statistical tests that will answer your statistical questions can be selected.

For example, your statistical question might be based on a hypothesis that there is a *significant difference* (this is a statistical term and should only be used in that context) between the effectiveness of two methods for teaching spelling to students at Year 3 level. The answers to your statistical questions are presented in the results section of your research report. After finding out the answers to your statistical questions, you then turn back to your original (substantive) research questions and provide *substantive answers* that communicate to readers the answers to your original (substantive) research questions, what the findings mean and later (in your discussion of your results) how they relate to the findings of previous research in the area. These consecutive steps can be summarised as follows:

- *substantive question* (the research question that you developed earlier and that points to the collection of quantitative data)
- **statistical question** (arising from your substantive question and related to your hypothesis)
- *statistical answer* to your statistical question (for example whether there is a (statistically) *significant difference* between scores on spelling tests completed by groups of students who experienced different methods of learning spelling)
- *substantive answer* to your substantive question.

Statistical question

Developed from original research questions that indicate a quantitative approach to the research. Statistical questions lead to statistical answers that then enable the original, substantive research question to be answered.

Here is an example. Note that the questions and answers could be phrased in other ways as well. Reference to Methods A and B could be replaced with more specific terms that denote the particular methods being compared.

- *Substantive question:* To what extent do spelling scores of Year 3 students in small, rural schools in (identify your state or county) using Method A differ from the scores of students using Method B?

Independent variable The variable the researcher manipulates in an experiment (or quasi-experiment). For example, by assigning some students to Method A and other students to Method B, or even exposing all students to one method and then to the other, the researcher aims to find out which method is more effective.

Continuous variables Associated with scores that can fall anywhere between the lowest and highest limits on a scale. Examples are pre-service teachers' levels of self-efficacy for solving particular mathematical problems, scores on tests and age in years/months. When a number of items are included in the scale, it is fitting to calculate statistical means (or mathematical averages).

Categorical variables Have distinct categories such as male/female or age range (rather than age in years and/or months)—for example, 20–29; 30–39. The numbers relate to categories only; they are not 'scores' and there is no attempt to calculate means from these numbers.

• *Statistical question:* Is there a *significant difference* in the spelling scores of Year 3 students in small, rural schools in (identify your state or county), depending on whether they are taught spelling using Method A or Method B?

• (One possible) *statistical answer* (depending on the results): Year 3 students in small, rural schools in (identify your state or county) who learn spelling using Method A achieve significantly higher scores in spelling than students using Method B.

• (One possible) *substantive answer* (depending on the statistical answer): Method A for learning spelling is more successful than Method B for Year 3 students in small, rural schools in (identify your state or county).

Types of variables

In the above example, the *approach to teaching spelling* is the **independent variable**. In this case, different methods for teaching spelling are compared for their ability to impact on the *dependent variable* (*accuracy in spelling*).

You will also need to be clear about whether your variables are **continuous variables** (as in the following example) or **categorical variables** (for example, male/female categories); this will be evident in your research question (for example, if you mention categories such as male/female).

In terms of continuous variables, Table 6.2 in Chapter 6 showed four items to which pre-service teachers responded on a six-point scale, indicating their confidence to solve spatial problems in mathematics. Respondents could choose anywhere along the scale that they felt was relevant for them. When the mean scores (or mathematical averages) for all four items for the variables are calculated across all responses, the result can be anywhere in between the lower and upper limits (1–6). If you were using these items or items that were constructed in a similar way, then you would enter into your spreadsheet a numeral from 1 to 6 for each item for each respondent. Scores on spelling tests or age in years/months (as opposed to age categories) are also continuous variables.

Ensuring that the variables are correctly classified and labelled enables the appropriate statistical tests to be performed on the data. When data are entered into SPSS, they need to be labelled so that the statistical program receives the correct instructions to do the calculations. It is also important to be clear about your conceptual framework. For example, if the research in your area indicates that gender or age is not important, then you would need to put forward strong arguments if you decided to include either of these variables. This is where it is important to be really clear about what information you need from your participants and not to collect information just because it could be useful.

Levels of measurement (nominal, ordinal, interval and ratio)
We have already touched on aspects of some of these levels in our earlier discussions. Knowing about different levels of measurement is important for interpreting your data.

A categorical variable such as male/female is an example of a *nominal level of measurement*. While you might assign numbers to genders (for example, 1 for male and 2 for female, or vice versa) for the purposes of entering data into your SPSS spreadsheet, you clearly categorise the variable so that analysis of the data will treat male/female as two categories of the same concept rather than as scores that are higher or lower than each other.

If you ask your participants to prioritise a list of points in order of their preferences, then 1 could be the point of highest preference and the highest number could represent the point least preferred by each respondent. In other words, participants *rank order* a list of items using an *ordinal scale*. This does not imply, however, that a respondent preferred Point 1 over Point 2 to the same degree that Point 2 was preferred over Point 3. The points are simply ranked in order of preference.

Interval levels of measurement are relevant to our spelling example. If there were ten items in the test, then it could transpire that some students will spell all of the words correctly and that it would also be possible for other students to obtain 9/10, 8/10 and so on as far as 0/10. The distance between 9/10 and 10/10 would be the same as for the distance between 1/10 and 2/10, but it would not be possible to conclude that a student who obtained 8/10 was twice as good at spelling as a student who obtained 4/10. This is because we are constrained by the test and its limitations. For example, even the student who obtains 0/10 can possibly spell some words, just not the ones on this particular test. The student who obtained 10/10 can likely spell other words as well. We do not know, of course, whether all or just some of the students who obtained 10/10 could successfully spell words that are more difficult than those included on the test. This means that while we can say that the students who all obtained 10/10 performed equally well *on the test*, we are unable to say conclusively whether they are all equally good at spelling more generally.

The *ratio scale* is difficult to achieve because, as well as having the capabilities of the interval scale, it is also possible to conclude that 4/10 is half as much as 8/10. This is because the starting point is zero. For example, you could conclude that, in a given timeframe, one student who walked 100 metres walked half as far as a student who walked 200 metres. You could also say that a student who completed a test in ten minutes did so in half the time that it took for another student who completed the test in twenty minutes.

Descriptive and inferential statistics

Broadly speaking, there are two basic types of statistics: *descriptive statistics* and **inferential statistics**. If all you need to do is to describe your sample in terms of the *mean* (or mathematical average) scores for your dependent variables, and perhaps the *mode* (the most frequently occurring score) and the *median* (the score in the middle if you listed all of the scores from highest to lowest or lowest to highest) for example, then you are using descriptive statistics. This is because you are describing the data set as it relates *only to the sample used in your study.*

The mean, the mode and the median are also referred to as **measures of central tendency**. Looking at these measures of

Inferential statistics go beyond describing the data for the sample of participants who took part in the study. Inferential statistics are able to determine the probability that the results for the sample are reflective of what might be expected in the broader population from which the sample was drawn. How the sample was chosen and its size are important for deciding whether inferential statistics are appropriate.

Measures of central tendency The mean, the mode and the median scores.

central tendency across the different groups in your study enables you to 'eyeball' what is happening. For example, you may observe that the mean score on an achievement test for a group that used a new method of learning spelling was higher than the mean score for a group that used the regular method or the mean score for males is higher than the mean score for females in some areas and vice versa in other areas. You might also observe whether most students' scores cluster around a particular level.

Descriptive statistics on their own cannot enable you to draw conclusions on any of the areas of interest about the population from which the sample was drawn. To do this would involve inferential statistics, in which case the way that the sample was chosen from the population would need to instil confidence that the sample was truly representative of the population. This is important because, in most small-scale studies, it is not possible to involve in the research all of the people who belong to the population of interest, such as all Year 3 students in all small rural schools in your state or county or, in many cases, a sample that is representative of the population.

If there exists a possibility that the sample is biased in some way, then the degree to which the sample differs from what would be found in the population when the dependent variables are measured would be greater than what could occur by chance. Different samples from the same population will vary to some extent in terms of how well the participants in the samples perform on the dependent variables; however, if the particular sample chosen is too different, then it is not possible to say that it represents the population. The *margin of error* when inferring from the sample to the population would simply be too great to be able to draw conclusions about the population with confidence. It would not be possible to say with an acceptable degree of confidence, therefore, that the differences in the mean scores between Method A and Method B for teaching spelling are *significantly different* and did not occur by chance. Returning to the substantive research question, it would not be possible to conclude that one method for teaching spelling is more effective than the other, and that the same conclusion could be reached if the entire population from which the sample was drawn was involved in the research.

In summary, inferential statistics enable you to use the findings to predict how other groups from the same population would perform using the two methods of learning spelling, or the *probability* that the results that you obtained from your sample are not only similar to the population but that there is a low probability that your results occurred by chance. Inferential statistics do not, however, enable you to predict how a particular individual from the same population will perform.

Statistical significance, probability and p-values

A number of statistical tests can determine whether there is a *significant difference* between two or more sets of scores associated with quantitative surveys or questionnaires, structured interviews and structured observations (as well as achievement tests). Each statistical test can only be used if certain conditions or assumptions are met.

We now return to the idea of the two methods of teaching spelling. We will leave aside for the moment how the sample was selected. Ideally, you would be able to go beyond the conclusion that the mean scores achieved by the classes using one method were simply higher than the mean scores achieved by classes using the other method. Instead, you may be able to conclude that the differences in the mean scores were of a magnitude that you could predict that the mean spelling scores for Year 3 classes in small, rural schools in your state or county would likely be *significantly* higher for classes taught using one method instead of the other. Alternatively, it could be appropriate to conclude that the methods were equally effective.

Of course, we are looking at groups of students here rather than individuals, but if a school needed to decide which method of teaching spelling to adopt for maximum effect with its Year 3 classes, then it would be helpful for the school to draw on research findings when making its decision. Part of its approach could also involve carefully monitoring the progress of all Year 3 students to determine whether applying the findings from the research works for its students. The school is also likely to think about how to work with students who do not perform the same as the group and to identify strategies for helping those students to achieve to the best of their ability. Knowing which method is likely to be better for the majority of students so that the approach is evidence-based, however, provides a good starting point for planning.

The question then becomes how certain the school can be that the findings from the research can be applied to their students. This is again where *probability* becomes important. It is not possible to be 100 per cent certain that all Year 3 classes across the state or county would do better if taught using the method that the research found was significantly more effective. There is always a *margin of error*, as no piece of research is perfect. For example, the spelling test is unlikely to be perfectly *reliable*. Statistics takes account of these situations. Researchers report the *probability (or p-value)*. For example, if the research found that classes taught using Method A achieved *significantly higher* mean scores than classes taught using Method B, the researcher would also report a p-value, such as $p < .05$. This means that there is at least 95 per cent chance that other Year 3 classes from the same population will also do better with Method A.

Statistical significance is also important for reporting *correlations*. For example, I found high positive correlations between pre-service teachers' levels of confidence to solve mathematical problems and their confidence to teach the same types of mathematical problems, such that, as the pre-service teachers' confidence in the first of these areas rose, so did their confidence in the other. The results for all areas were **statistically significant** ($p < .001$), meaning that there was just one in 1000 chance that the same correlation would not be found with other groups of pre-service teachers from the same

Statistically significant
When the results achieved on the dependent variable are at a level that could not have occurred by chance, for example when Method A is concluded to be more effective than Method B.

population. This is why it is important to describe the sample in terms of the population from which it came and how it was selected.

Your adviser will not expect you to know before your first consultation which statistical test/s you will need to conduct or which assumptions need to be met. It is also, therefore, not possible to make these decisions here. Despite this, a few tests that are commonly used can be mentioned. You can then do further reading on the tests if they are relevant to you. You can also have another look at some of the articles reporting quantitative research that you located for your literature review to find out which statistical tests and research designs they used to answer their research questions.

A caution to note when looking at these articles is that the research reported in them could be larger in scale than you are planning. Not all statistical tests will be relevant to your research. It is important to match the type of statistical test with the purpose of your research and your research design. You may find, however, that you can see connections with some of the points discussed above. After working with your adviser, you might be able to appreciate why the statistical test/s that you need to use are the same or different from the tests used in the research reported in your chosen evidence-based research articles.

Davies and Hughes (2014) summarise eight different types of tests of significance, relating to different types of correlations, different types of t-tests for different situations and tests that relate to different ways that the data are treated for the analysis. The choice of test depends not just on the purpose and design of your study, but also the types of variables (for example, continuous and/or categorical), the size of your sample and how it was selected.

If it is possible to make *inferences* about the population from which your sample was drawn, rather than to use *descriptive statistics* only, then that would be the optimal situation. You can discuss with your research supervisor, lecturer or guide whether this is possible in your situation.

Normal distribution

Occurs in the shape of a bell curve when the least number of scores falls at the extremes (very high and very low scores) and progressively more scores fall as we move closer to the centre of the distribution, which is where the mean and the median occur for a normal distribution.

Normal distribution

In your conversations with your research supervisor, lecturer or guide, it would be helpful to have a basic understanding of **normal distribution**. This is because a normal distribution is important for statistical inference and inferential statistics. Some statistical tests assume that the means from the sample are distributed normally. When scores are plotted on a graph to examine visually how frequently different possible scores occur, a normal distribution in the shape of what is colloquially known as a bell curve is produced when the least number of scores falls at the extremes (very high and very low scores) and progressively more scores fall as we move closer to the centre of the distribution, which is where the mean and the median occur for a normal distribution. We can see now why the mean, mode and median are often referred to as measures of central tendency.

Despite how frequently normal distributions are found, it is also surprising how commonly they are misunderstood. For example, we often hear of the *J-curve*, in which low scores are the most common through to high scores being the least common, incorrectly and colloquially referred to as a *bell curve*. An example of a J-curve is where more students achieve at the pass level than at the credit level, more students achieve at the credit level than at the distinction level and the number of students achieving distinctions is greater than the number of students achieving high distinctions. Such a distribution is commonly achieved through norm referencing, in which grades are awarded at least partly on a comparative basis with other students. Unlike a J-curve, a normal (or bell) curve is symmetrical in shape because of fewer scores falling at the extremes (highest and lowest scores) and most students tending to cluster around the mean.

The following exercise will help you to prepare for an early consultation with your research supervisor, lecturer or guide, and think about what you can do during and after the meeting.

For your notebook

Exercise 8.5 Consulting with your research supervisor, lecturer or another person regarding quantitative data analysis

Before your consultation:

- Ensure that you have a copy of your plans to take with you or to have ready for a teleconference or Skype meeting, including:
  - your topic
  - the purpose of your study
  - your broad and specific research questions and
  - your chosen research design and methods (including reasons for your choices).

- Find out whether you should send your notes around these points to your supervisor ahead of your meeting.

- Do further reading about the different methods of sample selection and their strengths and limitations, and prepare your case for your choice of sampling method.

During the consultation:

- Take notes.

- Ask clarifying questions as needed.

- Note any further work that you need to do or training that you can attend.

- Establish how frequently you should consult with your supervisor during this period of your study (noting that frequency is likely to vary, depending on your needs at each stage in the process).

Immediately after the consultation:

- Review your notes.

- Act on any advice given and/or note points to follow

through later as appropriate, including completing additional readings on research methods.

- Add any further comments to your notes.

- Seek clarification if needed, perhaps in a follow-up email when you thank the person who guided you or when you do your further reading or talk with another person.

Label your response 'Exercise 8.5 Consulting with your research supervisor, lecturer or another person regarding quantitative data analysis'.

 For your notebook

Exercise 8.6 Which statistical procedures were used in quantitative evidence-based research articles in your area of interest?

Return to the collection of *quantitative research articles* in your area of interest from Exercise 8.3.

Working with these articles, draw up and complete a table that summarises these reports and the statistical tests used as follows:

Area	Article 1 (author/year)	Article 2 (author/year)	Article 3 (author/year)
Abstract			
Key themes/main authors referenced			
Definitions/debates			
Research question/s			
Methods			
Sample size and selection			
Statistical tests or calculations			
Results or findings			

Area	Article 1 (author/year)	Article 2 (author/year)	Article 3 (author/year)
Implications			
Comments			

If you completed Exercise 4.4 from Chapter 4 in your notebook, you will have most of the above information and will just need to add the rows for *sample size and selection* and *statistical tests or calculations* for the quantitative research articles that you found. *If you can, note for each article whether inferential statistics were used.* (If you are unsure, then you can show the articles to someone with a statistical background. That person might be able to explain that point without going into too much detail.)

If you did not find any evidence-based articles that reported quantitative research, then this could be an opportunity to search the databases again to see whether you can locate any for this exercise.

Label your response 'Exercise 8.6 Which statistical procedures were used in quantitative evidence-based research articles in your area of interest?'

You are now in a good position to continue your discussions with your research supervisor, lecturer or other person helping you with your statistics. You will be able to engage in discussions about quantitative research previously conducted and reported in your area of interest. The key is to seek guidance early and to maintain contact so that your project planning sustains its momentum and you can reach important milestones such as submitting your research proposal and application for ethical clearance, collecting your data and submitting your research report within the specified timeframe. It is sometimes said that quantitative research requires more work in the planning stages, but a solid early effort will enable the data analysis to proceed more quickly than for qualitative research.

CONCLUSION: POINTS TO CONSIDER FOR MIXED-METHODS RESEARCH

Most small-scale research is either quantitative or qualitative, but occasionally novice researchers may be guided into mixed-methods research if that is more logical and provided that the research can still be kept as simple as possible. The decision depends as much on the background of the student and practical considerations such as the amount of time available to plan, conduct and report the findings as on the purpose of the research and the research question/s.

There are a number of considerations involved when planning mixed-methods research. The following questions provide a starting point for careful deliberation:

- Which comes first in the sequence, the collection of quantitative data or the collection of qualitative data? Why?
- Is one strategy more predominant than the other or are they of approximately equal weight?
- What is the relationship between the strategies? Does one build on the other? How?

Examples of methods and sequence include but are not limited to:

- developing and administering a quantitative survey, the results of which point to particular areas that need in-depth exploration with a smaller number of

participants using, for example, qualitative interviews
- commencing with qualitative interviews and/or observations to identify areas that are then incorporated into a follow-up quantitative survey with a larger number of participants.

Examining the logic behind a mixed-methods approach is similar to examining the logic behind research that is either quantitative or qualitative, but the task is much bigger. As implied in the questions above, the move to mixed methods does not just involve thinking about two strategies rather than one, but rather how they relate to one another and collectively address the purpose of the research and the research questions.

If you argue that your research questions will not be addressed with a single strategy, but you are advised by experienced researchers to use just one strategy, then there are several options that you could consider, depending on the nature of your questions.

In some situations, it is appropriate to plan research in several phases, one being quantitative and the other qualitative (or vice versa). You may need to convince your research supervisor that the findings from the first phase are important even without the findings from the second phase. In that case, it could be possible to argue that the research involves two phases, giving a broad outline of these phases and then explaining that, for the purposes of your small-scale study and your present assignment, the focus will be on one phase (usually the first phase). It is often good to conceive of research as something bigger than a one-off, small-scale study, albeit that your coursework may not have the space for you to complete more than one phase. Remember that the emphasis is not on conducting ground-breaking research that will have wide impact but on beginning the process of learning how to think systematically about problems that challenge you, interest you or make you curious in your professional life.

Whichever route you take, you will be asked to make convincing arguments for your choice. Even the first phase of a small-scale study—either quantitative or qualitative—needs to be worthwhile, and it needs to matter to someone.

REVIEW

It is now important to review your notes from the exercises in this chapter and your own developing research plan. The following concluding exercise focuses on making decisions (including tentative ones) about how you will analyse your data for your study.

CONCLUDING EXERCISE

 For your notebook

Exercise 8.7 Reviewing your notes and your plans

After reviewing your notes for each exercise in this chapter and revisiting your developing research plan, think about whether your plan is pointing to the collection of qualitative or quantitative data (or a combination of both).

- Examine the underlying logic between the parts of your plan, including the purpose of the research, the research question/s, the way that the sample will be selected, the proposed methods of data collection and possible methods or approaches to data analysis.

- Identify any further changes that need to be made to your plan.

- Present your plan to another student and/or your research supervisor for feedback.

Label your response 'Exercise 8.7 Reviewing your notes and your plans'.

CHAPTER SUMMARY

In this chapter, you took the time to:

- become familiar with a number of fundamental points related to qualitative research, including:
  - the nature of qualitative data
  - building theory inductively
  - challenges for qualitative researchers
  - connections between data collection and analysis
- examine the underlying logic between research questions, conceptual frameworks, data collection and analysis and presentation of research results and findings
- examine approaches to writing methods sections of qualitative research reports
- examine approaches used to analyse qualitative data and present the results
- find out what assistance in statistics is available to you as a student
- become familiar with a number of fundamental concepts related to quantitative research, including:
  - substantive and statistical research questions and answers
  - types of variables
  - levels of measurement
  - descriptive and inferential statistics

- – statistical significance, probability and p-values
- – normal distribution

• prepare for consultations with your research supervisor, lecturer or guide

• identify the statistical procedures used in quantitative research in your area of interest

• read definitions of important key terms: underlying assumptions, syntax, code book, statistical question, independent variable, continuous variables, categorical variables, measures of central tendency, inferential statistics, statistically significant, normal distribution.

TAKING IT FURTHER

Return to the list of references to research methods literature that you noted in Exercise 8.6.

• Take the time to explore the parts of these references that talk about analysing qualitative research data to take your thinking to deeper levels and to consider what might be useful for analysing your data.

• You may find the references to research methods literature (or updated versions) useful starting points for your further reading. The full bibliographic details are in the references at the end of the articles.

• Ensure you note the full bibliographic details of these references for future reference and even for your reference list in your research report, as appropriate.

• Note whether any of these references are available as e-books.

FURTHER READING

Davies, M. & Hughes, N. (2014), *Doing a Successful Research Project: Using qualitative or quantitative methods* (2nd ed.), Basingstoke: Palgrave Macmillan.

See Chapter 8, Chapter 9 and Chapter 14.

Ho, R. (2006), *Handbook of Univariate and Multivariate Data Analysis and Interpretation with SPSS*, London: Taylor & Francis.

Chapter 2 introduces readers to SPSS.

Wightman, L. & Moriarty, B. (2012), Lifelong Learning and Becoming a Mother: Evaluation of the Young Parents Program, *International Journal of Lifelong Education, 31*(5), pp. 555–67.

9

Thinking about findings and implications for practice and future research

This chapter will help you to:

 work towards the communication of the findings and implications of your small-scale research

 think about the extent of influence of small-scale research and its potential impact on participants.

Learning how to plan, conduct and report educational research is a lengthy and involved process. Each study that a novice researcher plans and implements offers the opportunity for further learning about the process. Undertaking a small-scale project within a limited timeframe and without access to funding and research assistants is a good place to start. It means being responsible for every step in the process—although there is guidance along the way. This experience is valuable, as there are many new skills to begin learning and to try for the first time. There also needs to be time in reserve to deal with delays and unexpected occurrences. Ensuring that the research is small-scale is imperative because research does not always go according to plan and more time could be needed on an ongoing basis than you might initially suspect.

Like many students, your first project might be your only one, but the experience will potentially change you professionally and for the better in ways that you might not anticipate. The process helps you to begin to think differently about how to approach problems in your professional life and about phenomena that make you curious or that challenge you—or should challenge you. What you once saw as simple may now appear quite complex, partly because you took the time to pause and to think over and over again where once you would have moved quickly forward. This is partly because you were challenged to define your own direction and to ask your own questions rather than to answer questions that others provided. The findings and implications for practice are important, but they can also go much deeper than answering your research question. After completing her small-scale study, a student once told me that she would never look at 'facts' the same way again, even those contained in departmental policy documents. Her experience of conducting her first study and discerning its findings had implications beyond what she anticipated.

Now is an ideal time to pause and to recheck the requirements of your subject or course to ensure that your work remains on track and that all prescribed conditions are met. This includes thinking about to whom the findings of the research could be important should they be communicated and your approach to working with your supervisor or lecturer while writing your research report. Consideration is then given to the extent of influence that the findings of a small-scale study can have on future practice and research, and the potential impact that research can have on participants during the project and beyond.

COMMUNICATING THE FINDINGS OF THE RESEARCH

Even though your study will be small-scale and the findings and implications may not initially extend far past the context in which the research is conducted, there is still value in the research, and this can occur in a number of ways. One such way is that, should the research be reported, other teachers who see synergies with the participant/s in the research or their context could be inspired to try something different with their own classes and to reflect on the impact. While the findings from a small-scale study will not change practice nationwide, they could help educators to *think differently about their practice*. This is unlikely to happen, however, if the study and its findings are not communicated or cannot for certain reasons be communicated beyond the assignment for which the research report is written. If there is an opportunity and it is appropriate to do so, however, the researcher could present the study and discuss its findings and implications at a professional development session or even at a staff meeting or professional conference. Perhaps, like Louise, the researcher could work with a mentor to take their work further and to proceed towards publication.

How and to what extent your research and its findings can be reported depends on the circumstances under which your data were collected, including the conditions attached to your course or subject in terms of ethical approval and other requirements. If, for example, your 'research' is part of your very early training and is an in-class project where class members are trialling among themselves a technique (for example, interviewing) and an instrument (for example, an interview schedule or interview guide), then it may not be appropriate or permissible to report the 'research' but to submit the work purely as an assignment. It is important, therefore, to check the parameters of your course with your class notes or lecturer in order to avoid any misconceptions about the purpose of your study and whether there are implications for reporting your research. It could be that the intention is to begin learning research processes ahead of undertaking other subjects or courses that involve or eventually lead to conducting a 'real' piece of research.

This is the point at which you may find it helpful to revisit your notes from Exercise 1.2 in Chapter 1, or to check the requirements of your current (later) course or subject.

 For your notebook

Exercise 9.1 Revisiting the requirements of your subject or course

Return to your notes from Exercise 1.2 and your course notes, and recheck:

- requirements and any parameters or restrictions for reporting the findings of your small-scale study

- the submission date for your report and any other important dates that precede it.

If you have already completed your research proposal and obtained ethical clearance to conduct your research, check the approval details again to ensure that you are meeting your obligations.

As you check the requirements and parameters for your research and reporting its findings, ask yourself and note your response to the question 'What conditions need to be met?' Keep these requirements close at hand for checking on an ongoing basis.

This exercise demonstrates the importance of the ongoing and consistent time commitment required to undertake research and to keep it on track and on schedule. Setting your studies aside for a while at any time during the planning, implementation and reporting of your research makes it difficult and time-consuming to pick up again. The process of thinking like a researcher and writing, if interrupted or cut short, has the potential to impact on the time available for reflecting on your findings and for discerning their implications for practice and future research once the data are collected and analysed. The following advice is helpful to consider before working through Chapter 10, which devotes considerable time to how to write your research report.

- Make sure that you build into your schedule time to write your report as the study progresses. Do not collect your data and then start writing your report. You will most likely run out of time.
- Each part of your research report requires different specific writing skills. Seek guidance before and during the writing of each part of the report and look again at how the different parts of the evidence-based research articles that you collected are written.
- If you completed a research proposal, then you will already have a good start to writing your research report. The literature review and methods sections

of the research proposal will be adapted and used for your final report.

- If you are writing an Honours or Masters thesis, your research report will be divided into chapters. Show your individual chapters to your research supervisor or lecturer for feedback at regular and agreed intervals, until you have a full draft of all chapters. Ensure that you look closely at a number of completed theses at your particular level for further guidance.

- It could be important to seek feedback on a small part of your writing (perhaps a couple of paragraphs) early so that you are aware of the high standards of writing expected in later drafts.

- Spend the time to prepare the best drafts of chapters that you possibly can before asking your supervisor for feedback. It is your task to edit your work and to write well, as it is *your* thesis or assignment. Keep an eye on your timelines, however, and do not delay submitting drafts longer than necessary, remembering that last-minute drafts may not align with your supervisor's other commitments.

- Take note of corrections and suggestions when you receive feedback (perhaps make a list of points) and ensure that issues around your early writing are not evident in later writing. Keep your list of points with you and refer to them when writing and proofreading. You could add to this list other points that you note from Chapter 10 that you also identify as important to you.

- If your writing is not of a suitable standard or you have had difficulty with academic writing in the past, look for and complete online or face-to-face courses on academic writing available at your university.

Following this basic advice enables your supervisor to spend more time responding to and discussing the quality of your ideas and your arguments as you write. This approach will also help to ensure that there is sufficient time to work on your findings, to discern their implications for future practice and research, and to meet your submission deadline. This means that you need to give priority to your study, to put in the required effort and time from the beginning and on an ongoing basis, and to initiate and negotiate regular contact with your supervisor. Avoiding periods when you do little or no work or do not contact your supervisor is paramount, although the frequency and regularity of meetings with your supervisor are likely to change across the period of your study according to the nature of your work at the time.

EXTENT OF INFLUENCE AND THE IMPACT OF RESEARCH ON PARTICIPANTS

In earlier chapters, you developed and revised several times key points about your proposed small-scale study. The latest version, recorded in Exercise 8.7, asked you to revisit your plan and to examine the underlying logic between the parts, including the purpose of the research, the research question/s, the way that the sample will be selected, the proposed methods of data collection and possible methods or approaches to data analysis. You then presented your plan to another student and/or your research supervisor for feedback.

Your first small-scale study is likely to be related to a challenge that you face in your current professional context or could face in the future. The findings could help you to think differently and more systematically about something that makes you curious professionally. The size of your sample and the way it is selected will impact how the findings of the study can be used and to whom they might be important.

If a small-scale study such as yours can be important to you, and perhaps important to your participants or your context, then it can be very valuable. *Inflating the value of the research* can occur, for example, if it is anticipated that the findings of a small-scale study, conducted over a very short period of time and probably with a small number of participants, is likely to make an impact nationally. If we uncover valuable information about exemplary teaching of creative writing by one teacher in a single, Year 3 class, the findings will not be of a magnitude that will change the way teachers across the country teach creative writing. Even so, novice researchers sometimes have the misconception during the early planning stages that their small-scale studies will have such a wide impact. It is important to remember that one small study will not provide conclusive *proof* about something, although it is important to remember the *cumulative effect* a number of small-scale studies can have in a particular area as the evidence builds. Your research could be part of that contribution.

The excitement that you bring to the project could be matched by the same excitement on the part of your potential participants, or you could be surprised about why everyone around you is not as excited as you are about your research. Others may not be able to place the same level of importance or priority on your study as you do.

A few possible reasons why potential participants may not be as excited as you could be connected to *what* you ask the participants to do or *when* you ask them to do it. Imagine that you identified a teacher who is regarded as exemplary in the teaching of creative writing and you enthusiastically suggest that you would like to observe the teacher in action, to have the teacher show you her planning documents and talk about what she does and how she does it. You also propose that the students and perhaps even the parents or other teachers might like to contribute their views so that you can learn as much as possible about this exemplary teacher, who you anticipate will be very keen to be involved. After all, it is recognition that her work is good. Perhaps the principal agrees to you approaching the teacher about your project to find out whether she would like to participate, but when you present your ideas to the teacher, there is not the gush of enthusiasm you expected. Perhaps you forgot to think about a range of possible reactions from and implications for the teacher.

Consider this. I wonder how many teachers in your school or your university classes feel comfortable working with children, but feel less comfortable teaching in front of adults. The teacher might have a feeling that she is being judged, even though you try to reassure her otherwise. Perhaps she is not as confident in her abilities as you seem to think. She could be worried about being observed as she teaches, or about the views of parents, students and other teachers being sought, in which case there would be ethical issues for you to consider as well as the scale of your project. It is also important to realise that including parents, students and other teachers in the study also makes them participants. The look on the teacher's face when you ask her to be your participant could be one of 'How do I say no?' Perhaps the research needs to be scaled back as it could exceed your small-scale limits and you may then also find that the teacher is happy to participate.

Another possibility for an apparent lack of enthusiasm from a potential participant could be because the teacher is very busy—perhaps she is studying at night like you and has an assignment due soon. Of course you try to reassure the teacher that she does not need to do any special preparation or spend any time in addition to what she would normally do to prepare for your observation, and you also promise that the interview will take no more than an hour before or after school. Yet it is reasonable to expect that the teacher might want to spend additional time in preparation just to ensure that everything goes smoothly, perhaps if she anticipates being a little nervous. There can be all kinds of reasons why your research is not as important to others as it is to you. Even if we stop and think about the teacher's perspective and the impact that the research could have on the teacher, it is easy to minimise in our minds what we anticipate will be the concerns of prospective participants.

It is equally possible that *ethical concerns can be downplayed*, arguing that any discomfort or possible feelings of embarrassment that could be experienced by participants will be outweighed by the contribution that the study's findings will make to knowledge and practice. Here we could be under-estimating the ethical concerns and inflating the value of the research, or both. Earlier, you considered to whom your research would be important. The researcher has a lot at stake and of course the research is important to the researcher, but the question is whether it is just as important to others. Thinking about the impact that taking part in research has on your participants could influence whether they and others around them would be prepared to be involved in other research in the future. It is important to consider the legacy you leave behind.

The next chapter will expand on a few of the points introduced in this chapter and consider other helpful hints around conducting and reporting research. Most of the emphasis in that chapter will be on the writing, given that each part of the research report has different expectations and requires different writing skills.

While everyone's experience of conducting research is different, it can be helpful to hear about other people's experiences. The following concluding exercises for your notebook provide the opportunity to learn about the experiences of other researchers and to reflect on those experiences as well as what you learned from this chapter.

CONCLUDING EXERCISES

 For your notebook

Exercise 9.2 Talking with people who have completed research

Find:

- one or two people who have conducted small-scale research
- one or two people who are more experienced researchers.

Ask these people to talk about their experiences and take notes. Focus on:

- what they found most rewarding and most challenging about planning, conducting and reporting their research
- what they found that was unexpected and how they dealt with these situations
- what they would do differently or how they would approach their research differently, given the benefits of hindsight
- what they would approach in a similar way if given another chance

- their experiences as participants in research—do they have any advice concerning the impact that research can have on participants?

 For your notebook

Exercise 9.3 Reviewing your notes from this chapter

Review the notes you took while working through this chapter, and your discussions and notes from Exercise 9.2.

Reflect and write about what you learned from your discussions and notes that could be important to you, particularly in terms of:

- any misconceptions that you may have had about the findings and implications associated with small-scale research

- making the most of the process and how your findings could be useful to you and to others

- points that you need to consider regarding the potential impact of research on participants during the research and into the future.

CHAPTER SUMMARY

In this chapter, you took time to review the requirements of your subject or course in order to:

- ensure that you remain focused and meet all of the prescribed conditions and timelines associated your course and research

- discern to whom the findings and implications of your research might be communicated.

You also took the time to think about:

- the time commitment needed to undertake the research, allowing sufficient time to work through and discuss the findings and possible implications for practice and future research

- the extent of influence that a small-scale study could have, to whom it is important and the impact of the research on participants.

You were also encouraged to consider how to:

- work towards the discernment and communication of the findings and implications of the research, and to

- help ensure that the research report is completed on time.

Finally, you took the opportunity to talk with people who had conducted small-scale research, including novice and experienced researchers, in order to learn from their experiences.

10
Conducting and reporting research

This chapter will help you to:

 consider practical issues about conducting research related to predicting timelines and communicating with stakeholders

 work on your academic writing skills and the writing of your research report.

Researchers can begin the process of planning their research by thinking about research questions that relate to problems in their professional contexts or problems that puzzle or challenge them, or about which they are curious. This is referred to as a *pragmatic approach*. Other researchers begin by thinking about the *paradigmatic approach* that they will take to their area of inquiry. Experienced researchers who begin with research questions and problems concurrently appreciate how their questions are situated paradigmatically or, at the very least, whether they are approaching the problem and their research questions from a quantitative, qualitative or mixed-methods perspective.

This book takes the pragmatic approach. Novice researchers, as well as many experienced researchers, often approach their research by foregrounding their research questions. We began the process in this book by constructing *draft research questions* that reflected our particular areas of professional interest or problems that we wanted to investigate. Then, when we explored what was known about our area of interest through examining previous research and how it was conducted (the *literature review*), we were able to refine our research questions further based on what was already known. To do this we used the skills around *research question construction* that we had already started to learn. The process of developing research questions was *iterative* because the questions were refined further as we made connections between the research questions and previous research literature, the research design and methods for answering the research questions, ethical issues/concerns and, later, *paradigms*. The process was also iterative because it provided multiple opportunities to learn more about how to construct good research questions. Good research questions are the means by which the components of the research hold together: they underpin the research design and methods, an ethical approach and an understanding of paradigms. A logical line of thought therefore connects all parts of the plan, regardless of how the researcher starts the process of planning the research.

The connections between the research questions and the other parts of a research plan or research proposal are also expected to be evident in the reporting of the research. You already examined written reports of research in your area of interest, mainly as articles but perhaps also as theses or other reports. Regardless of whether the research and its findings are disseminated through a presentation, an article or a thesis, the underlying logic between the research questions, the review of literature, the design and methods adopted and the presentation of the results and/or findings is paramount. Readers and examiners of reported research expect to see this alignment. Without it, the research design could be flawed—perhaps to a point where it can be difficult to retrieve logic later and build that logic into the research report.

This chapter commences by focusing on practical issues related to conducting research, specifically around predicting timelines and communicating with participants and potential participants. This discussion again helps to highlight the importance of thinking small scale as a novice researcher, and keeping time in reserve for unexpected delays and occurrences.

The chapter then moves its focus to the writing of the research report and aspects of academic writing skills. After providing an overview of the sections in a research report and related exercises for your notebook, it then focuses on a technique that I developed for, and provide to, students to check the content and sequencing of their academic writing. This technique enables students to scrutinise their draft reports or other academic writing using processes of deconstruction and reconstruction, helping to ensure that all the required parts of the paper are present and repetition is avoided. The technique is also a good first line of attack if you are well over or well under the specified word count for your assignment or report.

The chapter finishes with some concluding thoughts about the approach taken in this book. It provides some final pieces of advice for novice researchers and reinforces the value of small-scale research.

PREDICTING TIMELINES AND COMMUNICATING WITH PARTICIPANTS

It is important to be as organised and as prepared as possible when conducting research and to have a schedule of events in the research cycle that is revisited often. Even then, research does not always proceed as planned. Common misconceptions are that *unexpected events* are rare, that *timelines* are relatively easy to predict and that *communication with participants* is straightforward.

Unexpected events are commonplace. When they occur, you may find that your participants need to prioritise what is important to them and/or their students or staff. Such events can affect the researcher's timelines. Being aware of possible contingencies and building in sufficient time to resolve issues around unexpected events helps to ensure that the project is successful and the findings and implications for future practice and research are meaningful.

A number of unexpected events occurred during the data collection for my PhD. There were mail delays that affected the receipt of important documents by one of the schools, bus and train strikes (I was dependent on public transport), electrical power failures (I needed power to take video footage) and, for the first time in 60 years, the teachers in the state went on strike (I had seven teachers and their classes involved in the research). These events all occurred within the second ten-week period of data collection. Fortunately, I had a spare copy of the documents with me when I arrived at the school and found that the original documents were delayed in the mail. The principal, who was a PhD graduate, was most obliging and helped me to make further copies of the documents for use that day. I called on favours from relatives to drive me to the schools on the days when the trains and buses were on strike and I renegotiated the dates for the video footage. Some teachers decided not to strike, but those who did offered to work around one or more of the original dates for data collection. I managed to keep the data collection overall within the original specified time limits, although there were a few anxious moments along the way.

These experiences are examples of how research does not always proceed according to plan, and they show the importance of building into the schedule sufficient time to deal with unexpected events. If not handled carefully, unexpected events can affect your schedule and leave you with insufficient time to think deeply about the findings and implications of the study and, ultimately, to complete your research report on time and to an acceptable standard.

Timelines can be difficult to predict. For example, you may visit a site to meet with potential participants to explain your research or to work with participants. On arrival, you find that one of the teachers has gone home ill or there is an emergency in the school and all plans that teachers made for the afternoon are cancelled. You then need to go back to your schedule and renegotiate, or add these items to your next scheduled visit to the school. If there is an emergency at the data-collection site, then even your renegotiation of times may need to be done later. While it is important to have a schedule, the longer the period of data gathering, the more chance there is that something unexpected will happen and the less chance there is that you can reschedule events to fit in with your overall timeline. In summary, you need to remember that there could be times when your participants are unable to prioritise your research.

Regular *communication with participants* and other stakeholders is crucial, as long as you do not over-burden them. Having a smaller number of participants than you think that you can manage can often be beneficial for all parties. It enables you to spend the amount of time needed to provide support. For example, if your research requires teachers to work in ways that are unfamiliar to them, then they may have concerns about doing what you ask if you do not allow sufficient time to discuss the requirements or you do not stay in regular communication. If your schedule is too tight, it could be difficult for teachers to discuss points or ask questions that could determine whether the research is conducted as planned, and even whether participants are able to remain in the study. If the study becomes too much of a burden for participants, your sample could diminish and your original plans not be achieved.

Communication with participants also needs to be respectful. You should not be respectful just for the purpose of achieving your own aims; you should be genuinely respectful in any case. This respect starts with the period when you are planning your research and recruiting participants, to data gathering and the communication of the findings of the study, including consideration of the implications of the findings for practice and future research.

When planning your research and developing your research proposal, you will be required to provide timelines and a schedule showing the sequence and timing of the main tasks. The following exercise for your notebook provides the opportunity to develop or check your timeline and to step yourself through the tasks associated with your research, including locating or constructing data-gathering instruments, making initial contact with potential participants and their supervisors, and completing data collection and analysis. Time also needs to be built in for completing transcripts soon after each interview or inputting numerical data as appropriate, data analysis and writing drafts of sections of the research report progressively. Backward mapping from the due date for your report and building in more time than you might think is necessary for writing the final parts of your report, revisiting and modifying parts of the report already drafted and preparing the presentation of the document for final submission are all very important.

 For your notebook

Exercise 10.1 Predicting timelines and communicating with participants

Revisit your developing research plan. If you have not already done so, produce a schedule showing each task and when each task will be completed.

Talk through your schedule and your timelines with another student or your research supervisor. Remember to take account of the number of participants, distances to travel, where you will collect your data, and the number and duration of visits to your data-gathering sites. Note the lengths of interviews or observations as appropriate.

Consider your participants:

- What are you asking of them?
- Does it sound realistic in terms of their time commitment?

Brainstorm possible problems or events that could delay your plans. What contingencies have you built in should they be needed? (Note that it is not possible to predict these events ahead of time. This part of the exercise helps you to consider whether your timeline is able to accommodate unexpected delays or events.)

THE RESEARCH REPORT

In reading reports of research in articles and other places, you will have noticed that the sections in a research report have a typical structure, although there are differences of a more minor nature between different reports. All research reports have a title, an abstract, a section in which the research problem and context or background are introduced and a literature review section (sometimes the introduction or background section and the literature review are combined in an article), a results section (particularly if the research is quantitative) and/or a findings section. The findings are discussed, sometimes in a section called 'Discussion'. The implications of the findings for future research (and sometimes practice) are also discussed at the end.

Before reading the notes on each part of a research report below, gather the articles that you collected for your literature review so that you can interrogate the different parts of selected articles after you read the points below and complete the 'For your notebook' exercises that appear along the way. The exercises, including the questions that they ask you, and the text preceding them will help you to understand what needs to be included in each section of a research report. You have the opportunity to scrutinise research as it was reported in articles that you identified for review in your area of interest. The exercises also help you to begin to see how research is evaluated and what examiners look for in research reports, and to consider what could be important for writing the report of your research. It is always helpful to anticipate how others could evaluate your research and your research report. The exercises for your notebook in this section will help you to begin to think about these points in advance.

Title, abstract and keywords

The title and the abstract of the report need to be tightly written and informative. The titles and abstracts help potential readers to decide whether research reports are relevant before downloading and reading them. Every word needs to count. Readers are often led to research reports by keywords. This means that if titles and abstracts contain words and phrases that are not necessary, there is less room for words that point to the focus and nature of the research.

Research reports will often also include a short list of keywords underneath the abstract. When potential readers use keywords relating to what they are looking for then carefully worded titles and abstracts and carefully chosen keywords individually and together can be very effective in locating relevant published research. Journals are very strict about maximum word counts for abstracts. A loosely worded abstract is likely to run short on words before all of the required features expected in an abstract can be added.

Title

The title of the research report is generally quite short. Titles that are too long should be avoided. Many titles use a colon to divide the title into two parts, consisting of a title and sub-title. A problem with some titles is that one part of the title (often the first part leading to the colon) is creative but not informative and, when the title is carefully examined, it could be concluded that the first part adds nothing to conveying the focus of the research or how it was conducted. The option is to consider whether the sub-title is all that is needed or whether the title (the first part before the colon) could be replaced with other words that are more effective and informative. Not all research reports that are published have tight and informative titles, and you may have seen some that fall into that category. The tip here is to do some further reading about what makes a good title and to examine a number of titles to see whether you can discern what makes some titles better than others. Just because a paper is published does not mean that the paper is exemplary in every way. Another tip is to use good titles as exemplars rather than to take your lead from very creative but less effective titles.

Abstract

There are several places where you can get guidance about what to include in the abstract. The first is your course or subject notes and criteria sheet or marking rubric for the assignment (if provided). You could find that the notes are very specific about what needs to be included in the abstract to satisfy requirements.

It is important to know which publication manual or style guide you are required to follow. Many students in education will find that they are required to follow the American Psychological Association (APA, 2010) publication manual, but it could be one of the other style manuals available. The APA style manual lists the content requirements for abstracts, depending on the type of article or research report. Most typically, abstracts will address the purpose of the research, key points about the methods and participants, key results and findings, and the implications of the findings for future research and sometimes for practice.

It is important to check the maximum word count allowed for the abstract. The word count varies from one journal to another (see the notes for contributors if you are working towards publication), but all are quite short. Abstracts for conference presentations are often quite a bit longer because delegates at the conference then have sufficient information to decide which presentations that are offered concurrently are most relevant for them to attend. Course or subject notes are also likely to specify the word limits for the abstract in the research report. In addition to ensuring that the word limit is not exceeded for theses and other research reports that are submitted for assignments, it is advisable to keep the abstract on a single page.

Keywords

If keywords are required, the number will usually be specified, such as five to six keywords. The aim of the keywords for published articles and papers is that potential readers and other researchers will search for articles using keywords and that the keywords that are used by researchers in your field will lead them to your article.

One way to test your keywords is to put them, one at a time and in combination, into a search engine or even into Google Scholar to see how many references appear. If thousands or even hundreds of papers are found using your keywords, then your keywords or combination of keywords will need to be more specific. Even if you are not intending to proceed towards publication, the same general principle applies.

 For your notebook

Exercise 10.2 Examining the title, abstract and keywords of research reports

After highlighting or noting the key features of research report titles, abstracts and keywords above, select three or four articles reporting research that you included or considered for inclusion in your literature review.

Explain in your notebook the strengths and/or points that could be improved for the title of each article. Place this information on a table or note your points in dot point form for ease of reference.

Use the keywords (if they are included in those articles) to do searches of library databases or Google Scholar to see whether those articles are found when the keywords are used singularly or in combination. How well did the keywords work for locating the articles?

Start drafting some possible titles and keywords for your research report. You can put these aside until later when you can review them again as you get into your research and commence writing. It sometimes takes many attempts before the title, in particular, is the one that you will use. Revisit the ideas about titles provided above and your notes from this exercise as you do this work.

INTRODUCTION/LITERATURE REVIEW

These sections of the research report are sometimes presented as one section and sometimes separately in articles. The introduction and literature review always appear after the abstract (and after the keywords if keywords are included), and they can be given different headings. For example, the introduction could be referred to as the background or context, and the literature review could be referred to as the review of literature or it could be included with the background or introduction section. Other variations are also possible but they are very similar to the suggestions here. It is not advisable to be too creative because research reports are written in predictable ways so that readers can concentrate on the content of sections that they are expecting to appear in a certain way rather than to be side-tracked or distracted unnecessarily. It is important to check your course notes for specific requirements or the notes for contributors if preparing an article or other report for possible publication.

The introductions and literature reviews for theses appear as Chapters 1 and 2. There is more room to cover a wider area in the literature review in a thesis compared with an article. This means that research reported in articles is more focused and the literature review is shorter in length. It will concentrate on the most relevant literature and is very likely to use a smaller number of references across a narrower range.

The research questions often appear at the end of the literature review or at the beginning of the methods section. Either way, it should be clear how the research questions relate to previous research and guide the present study.

 For your notebook

Exercise 10.3 Examining the introduction and literature review sections of articles

Returning to the articles that you located from your literature review, examine the structure of the introduction/literature review sections.

- What structure did these reports use? Did the introduction and literature review appear as one section or two and what heading/s were used?

- Where are the research questions or focus of the study provided?

- Is it clear how the research questions and focus or purpose of the research relate to what was found in previous research in the area?

METHODS (OR METHODOLOGY) SECTION

This section of the research report will closely follow the same section in the research plan or proposal. The methods section in a proposal is written in future tense because the research is still to be conducted, whereas the methods section in a research report is written in past tense. If you are submitting your report as an assignment rather than as a thesis, you may find that the methods section is almost identical to the methods section in the proposal. The main differences could relate to the tense and responding to questions or feedback from the examination of the proposal. Again, it is important to check your course notes in case there is anything else that needs to be added. Looking at other research reports, such as articles and theses, can also be helpful. For example, these other reports could lead you to research methods literature that you find helpful but had not already located.

The methods section of your final report can be prepared while the research is being conducted. It is often also easier to complete the methods section during the process because you are able to remember the finer detail more easily at the time. Ensure that the key points about your methods are clearly conveyed in the methods section. This would usually include how the data were analysed. The sequencing of information needs to be logical and the writing should be clear and succinct. This section should not be longer than necessary and readers need to be clear about what you did. There needs to be enough detail for readers to know how the research could be replicated.

For your notebook

Exercise 10.4 Examining the methods sections of research reports

Check the methods sections of the articles that you gathered to determine their clarity. Note what information is provided, such as the number of participants and so forth.

Is the sequencing of information logical and is similar information (for example about the participants) kept together?

Would you know how to design a study the same as this one based on the information provided?

RESULTS AND/OR FINDINGS

Theses often have a results chapter and a separate findings or discussion of the findings chapter. Other research reports could also have separate sections for the results and for the findings. You will again be guided by your supervisor and course notes or notes for contributors or other articles in the same journal if preparing an article or other publication for consideration. Where they are in two sections or in two chapters, the results and findings have specific foci. The results section does not discuss the findings or show how the findings are consistent with, different from or add to previous research conducted in the area. In quantitative research, tables that report the results of statistical tests are usually a strong feature whereas the results section of a qualitative research report will draw on data such as direct quotations from participants—for example, from interviews. It is common to report the results under the research questions that guided the study. The results section does not discuss or further interpret the results, or speculate as to the reasons for the results. It is also left to the findings or discussion of the findings section to situate what was found in light of earlier research. This could include explaining how the findings are consistent (or not) with previous research. In qualitative research, it is also acceptable to introduce (a limited amount of) literature that was not used in the literature review and that only later was found to be relevant. This does not always occur, however.

DISCUSSION/CONCLUSION

The heading for the last part of your research report will depend on the content of the previous sections as well as the last section. Sometimes the discussion of the findings leads into the identification and discussion of implications for future research and practice, and sometimes these latter points are found in a separate conclusion. It is not possible to determine here which way you should proceed; again, it is important to go back to your course notes and even look at how the articles that you included in your literature review went about presenting the final sections of their reports. Another important influence is the word count, which might also help you to determine how many separate sections will be in your report. It is a good idea to estimate ahead of time roughly how many words will be in each section so that you do not include too many ideas in previous sections and then find that your word count is exceeded before you write the final parts of your report.

For your notebook

Exercise 10.5 Examining the results, findings and discussion sections of research reports

Examine the sections of your chosen research articles that appear after the methods sections. Compare and contrast across the three or four articles how these final parts of the articles are organised and the headings that are used. If you have a selection of quantitative and qualitative research reports, how are the approaches used within and across these traditions similar or different?

Which approaches seem to be most relevant to the type of research that you are planning to conduct and report? What might your headings for these sections possibly be and what would they each contain?

REFERENCES

The reference list is one section of the research report that can and should be compiled progressively, rather than left until the end. An accurate reference list depends on having complete bibliographic details about each reference used and following systematically and in minute detail the requirements of the referencing system that you are obliged to follow. This is very tedious work, and it is easy to overlook simple points such as which parts in article titles and journal titles need to be in upper/lower case and which are italicised. Even the number of spaces after punctuation is important. If you use a system such as EndNote for compiling your reference list, there is still no substitute for knowing the relevant reference system well and keeping a copy of the manual at your side as you compile and check the reference list.

My suggestion is to add each reference to the reference list as it is used. This approach avoids the need to search for books and articles again at the end because you do not have all the bibliographic information. If you have some references that you have not yet decided whether to use, you can still add them to your list. You might, however, shade them in a different colour until you make your decision so that you do not inadvertently include any references that are not used in the text. A reference list (as opposed to a bibliography) includes all of the references used in the text and the items in the reference list are *all* found in text. APA is so complex that you really need an opportunity to go through your list a number of times before submitting your report. You are better placed to do this and to identify inconsistencies if the list is constructed progressively rather than at one time at the end. On the few occasions that I have left it to the end to construct my reference list, I have regretted my decision, as time always seems to be in short supply towards the end.

APPENDIX/APPENDICES

Just like the reference list, items in appendices need to be referred to in the text, and extra appendices that are not part of the report should not be included. APA provides further assistance with appendices and answers questions such as how to label them. In fact, it is worth spending time reading different parts of the APA manual (or other specified style guide) to familiarise yourself with the help that it provides and its specific requirements in a number of areas. Many areas are covered; students often have the view that APA is important for in text referencing and reference lists only.

ACADEMIC WRITING: CHECKING CONTENT AND SEQUENCE

The technique introduced here for analysing the content and sequence of your draft report or other academic writing is a good starting point for proofreading your work. Starting with this bigger picture analysis before checking the grammar and other more detailed technical points in your writing could save you time because some of the passages that you scrutinise carefully first when analysing your work for content and sequence could be removed or placed elsewhere in your document or other sentences added. It is therefore more efficient to ensure that the content and sequencing are right first so that you can then check the work that remains in closer detail.

The technique that I use to help students check the content and sequence of their writing appears as a list of steps in the left column of Table 10.1. The column on the right provides explanatory notes for some of the ideas.

Table 10.1 Steps for checking the content and sequence of academic writing

Steps for checking your paper	Comments on the steps
1 **Print on one side of the paper only.**	To complete this exercise you need to have all parts of the paper in front of you simultaneously and without the need to turn pages over or scroll up and down the screen.

Steps for checking your paper	Comments on the steps
2 **Write in the margin next to each paragraph the topic covered in that paragraph.** If you identify two topics, then note them both. (Adjustments will need to be made later).	A common error in writing is that there are two topic sentences at the start of a paragraph. The third and later sentences in the paragraph then often expand on the topic in the second sentence, leaving the topic introduced in the first sentence without discussion or expansion. Later in this process, there is the opportunity to decide whether both topics are important and then to make adjustments as needed.
3 **Check the topic of each paragraph with the heading under which it currently sits.** If the paragraph does not relate to the heading, remove that paragraph and place it aside or make a note in the margin. Have a look at the other headings in the paper and see whether the paragraph belongs elsewhere, moving it if necessary. If not, discard it or place it elsewhere just in case you change your mind later.	This step assumes that you are following closely the requirements of the assignment. Keep those requirements beside you as you write and proofread your paper. You may even find that the paragraphs fit what you were asked to do, but that the heading for that section of the paper needs to be adjusted to be consistent with the requirements of the task.
4 **Check for repetition within and between sections.** If you find any repetition, decide where the topic needs to be discussed and take all information to that place. Ensure that there is no repetition, cull and condense as necessary. Brief, passing reference to the same concept may be all that is needed later if at all.	Another common problem with writing is that not all the same material is kept together. Once we identify all the sentences or paragraphs that relate to the same topic and put them together and under the appropriate heading if they are currently under different headings, we can see what we have and identify whether there are gaps or any repetition. This part of the technique can be helpful for increasing or reducing the word count if it is a problem.

Steps for checking your paper	Comments on the steps
5 **Check any paragraphs where you identified more than one topic.** If you have not already removed or discarded parts, check these paragraphs and make decisions.	If both topics are important, then what was previously one paragraph may become two paragraphs, each dealing with one topic. Students who are under the specified word limit for their assignment may find that they are no longer under the limit if they need to make these adjustments.
6 **Check the sequencing of paragraphs within sections and the sequencing of the sections.** They need to be logical. Reposition any paragraphs that are out of sequence or not consistent with the assignment description. Some paragraphs may now appear not to be relevant and so would be discarded.	You could also find after completing this step that there are one or more missing paragraphs that need to be written in between the others so that the sequence of topics is logical and complete. Again, this could effectively increase the word count if the paper is under the minimum number of words specified.
7 **Now read through the paper as a whole, then repeat Steps 1-6.** Once you remove irrelevant or repeated material, you can see things much more clearly. You can check whether you have covered everything and need to add anything or whether there is still repetition.	You can also decide whether some words or phrases that start or end paragraphs or sections need altering—even slightly—so that they fit the changes made through using this technique.

For your notebook

Exercise 10.6 Checking the content and sequencing of your writing

For this exercise, you will check the content and sequencing of a paper or part of a paper that you wrote. If you completed your literature review earlier (or a draft of your literature review), that writing could be the focus for this exercise.

Work through the seven steps in the technique described above with your sample writing.

Then read through your latest version of your writing and compare it with your earlier attempts. In what way is your latest version different from your earlier versions?

CONCLUDING THOUGHTS

One of the first pieces of advice that novice researchers are often given about writing their research reports is to *begin the writing early and to write the report progressively*, rather than to wait until the data are collected and analysed. Writing is an intensive process: even many experienced and highly accomplished writers describe the process of writing as difficult and attest to the amount of time that it takes to produce a good piece of writing. Writing the different parts of the research report or thesis progressively and also building in time after the data are analysed and well before the report is due mean that there is time to revisit earlier writing, employ the technique introduced in this chapter, and ensure that the document is completed on schedule and finished to a high standard.

Good writing is more than writing correctly. It is important to reach high standards in terms of the technical aspects of writing, including grammar and syntax, but really mature writing goes beyond what could be achieved by using the technique for checking the content and sequence of the report or by using correct grammar. One reason why it is a little easier for experienced writers to write well and at a mature level is because they have been working in their particular areas of research interest for considerable time. Each time that writers work on another paper in the same area, the writing is likely to become more mature, reflecting a similar process with their thinking.

Even after familiarity with the area is gained and decisions are made about the content to be covered within even one part of the research report, it is not always a simple matter of following through with the writing plan. Just as developing research questions is an iterative process that sees the questions change and become more refined over time, writing is also an iterative process, in which the writer might start with a plan, begin writing to the plan but then find the need to modify the plan as the writing progresses. It is not until the writing of a section of the report or other piece of academic writing commences that discoveries about how to approach that part of the writing really begin to take shape as the plan is tested.

Paragraphs can also be quite simple or very difficult to write. Writers commonly find that some paragraphs are relatively easy, especially once they make a good start with writing that part of the paper, but other paragraphs are more difficult and take a lot more time than anticipated. Still other paragraphs appear to be working well on the day that they were written but on rereading the next day are found to be perhaps not as clear as previously thought. Some sentences within the paragraph are written and rewritten using trial and error, experimenting with different approaches until clarity is reached. It is clear that a considerable amount of time needs to be set aside for writing.

Another important point to consider is the range of skills needed to write the different parts of a research report. The specific skills required to write a tight abstract that includes all of the necessary information are quite different from the skills needed to write the results section in a quantitative research report, which is also very different from writing the results or findings sections of a qualitative study. The Further Reading section at the end of this chapter lists three books that you will find useful. Pyrczak's (2017) book is recommended not only for evaluating research articles but also for writing the different parts of a research report. Also listed is Piercy (2014), which is recommended for working on grammar. It deals with common problems, not all of which are widely known. Finally, the American Psychological Association's *Publication Manual* (6th ed.), commonly referred to as the 'APA Manual', is listed because it is a worthwhile accompaniment to any serious student's library and is especially worthwhile for postgraduate students, although not just for the reasons for which it is most commonly known or consulted. Aside from providing detailed information about how to reference (both in text and the reference list) using the APA, which is a common requirement in our discipline, the APA Manual provides information on a wide range of areas related not only to the presentation of research reports and other academic papers, but also to academic writing more generally, including when to use first or third person, the use of personal pronouns and tense. Commonly regarded as a reference book, the APA Manual is much more.

This chapter reinforced the approach taken to planning and conducting small-scale research introduced in the first chapter and followed throughout the book. The final suggestion is *not to rush the process* —particularly the first part, where the topic and problem are identified and the iterative process for developing good research questions begins. Novice researchers cannot start or finish at the point reached by PhD graduates, but for both working more slowly and carefully at the start of the planning process often leads to picking up momentum later. Small-scale studies, carefully planned and executed, can help novice researchers and others to think more deeply and systematically about how to approach problems in their professional contexts. These skills are needed and, as a result of increasingly challenging and changing professional environments, are becoming increasingly valued. If small-scale research is disseminated, other practitioners might see similarities between the research context and their own professional context, and be inspired to think differently about their practice. Novice researchers might even continue learning about research beyond this level and, through undertaking further training and research, become part of a broader research community.

CHAPTER SUMMARY

In this chapter, you took the time to:

- think about issues relating to setting timelines and communicating with research participants or other stakeholders

- consider how research reports are structured and the features of different sections in a research report

- trial a technique for checking the content and sequencing of ideas when writing an academic paper

- think about why it is important to write research reports progressively, rather than to start writing after the data are collected and analysed.

FURTHER READING

American Psychological Association (2010), *Publication Manual* (6th ed.), Washington, DC: American Psychological Association.

Piercy, J. (2014), *The 25 Rules of Grammar: The essential guide to good English*, London: Michael O'Mara Books.

Pyrczak, F. (2017), *Evaluating Research in Academic Journals: A practical guide to realistic evaluation* (6th ed.), Glendale, CA: Pyrczak Publishing.

GLOSSARY

Action research A process of systematically examining one's own practice, using a cycle of planning, acting, observing and reflecting.

Annotated bibliography A list of references presented just like a reference list, with a summary paragraph outlining each item under its entry.

Anonymity Not revealing the identities of the participants in your research.

Case A complete entity that is distinctive in its own right. A small-scale study is likely to focus on a case that is close to home, such as a teacher, a school, a program or a class rather than an educational or cultural organisation, an institution or a nation. Cases are also described by type, such as different types of single case studies or a multiple case study.

Categorical variables Have distinct categories such as male/female or age range (rather than age in years and/or months)—for example, 20–29; 30–39. The numbers relate to categories only; they are not 'scores' and there is no attempt to calculate means from these numbers.

Code book A collection of instructions (syntax) for analysing data in SPSS.

Conceptual or theoretical framework Consists of the themes that you drew from your reading of the reports of previous research and related literature. The literature review is shaped around these themes.

Confidentiality Closely related to anonymity. Selected data in the form of words are often used in the research report, although to maintain confidentiality, participants' words are usually presented anonymously or using pseudonyms, unless there is prior agreement.

Continuous variables Associated with scores that can fall anywhere between the lowest and highest limits on a scale. Examples are pre-service teachers' levels of self-efficacy for solving particular mathematical problems, scores on tests and age in years/months. When a number of items are included in the scale, it is fitting to calculate statistical means (or mathematical averages).

Convenience sample Made up of people who are easy to reach, available, convenient or close to hand.

Correlation Refers to the statistical relationship between two or more concepts or variables. It looks for patterns of association but cannot test for cause and effect.

Data The evidence or information collected in order to answer the research question/s.

Data-collection instruments Used to collect data from the participants in a study. They may include surveys or questionnaires, achievement tests, interview schedules or interview guides and observation schedules.

Deductive analysis Begins with a theory and collecting data to test the theory. Working deductively to test theory is usually associated with quantitative research.

Dependent variables Variables that are measured. For example, achievement in spelling could be measured by administering spelling tests to students working in Method A and Method B so that the methods of teaching spelling (the independent variable) can be compared.

Descriptive statistics Calculated on quantitative data and describe that set of data—for example, using percentages, means (mathematical averages), median (the score that is in the middle if you lined up all scores from all participants on a variable from highest to lowest or vice versa) and mode (the most frequently occurring score), as appropriate. Descriptive statistics are unable to be used to predict how other cohorts (of students, for example) might perform in similar situations, as is the case with inferential statistics.

Edited books Different from authored books because the editor or editors are not the authors of all of the chapters. They may write one or more chapters, but most chapters will be written by other researchers who may be known for their expertise. It is important to make the distinction between edited and authored books in lists of references or when researchers list their publications.

Educational research Involves a planned and systematic investigation or exploration of a problem or issue. The findings can help to inform practice and further research.

Effect size Reports the extent to which the variable of interest accounts for differences in achievement in students who are exposed to that method, compared with students who are not exposed to that method, for example. By implication, the difference that is not found to be attributable to the variable of interest must be attributable to other variables.

Ethics in practice Refers to the ethical considerations that arise during the conduct of research and that require the researcher's attention at the time.

Ethnography The study of groups over a period of time through immersion in the field and a variety of research methods for the collection of data.

Evidence-based research articles Typically found in academic journals and include a title, abstract (summary of the research), critical review of previous research in the area, methods section detailing how the study was conducted, results and/or findings section based on analysis of the data collected, discussion section and conclusions about where the research could go next or how the findings could be relevant to practitioners, and a reference list.

Experiment Experimental and quasi-experimental designs have some features in common but only (true) experiments randomly allocate participants to the control and experimental groups. In schools, the need for classes to remain intact usually means that quasi-experiments are used.

Focus group interview In focus groups, participants are generally invited to attend, and are encouraged by the interviewer to interact with each other rather than respond to the interviewer only.

Hypothesis Prediction about the findings of a study that is proposed at the start of the research. Generally influenced by previous research and theory, and usually relates to quantitative research, in which data are in the form of numbers.

Independent variable The variable the researcher manipulates in an experiment (or quasi-experiment). For example, by assigning some students to Method A and other students to Method B, or even exposing all students to one method and then to the other, the researcher aims to find out which method is more effective.

Inductive analysis The way that the researcher moves from the data collection through to the identification and discussion of the themes or patterns that emerge from the analysis of the data. Researchers use different strategies depending on their particular study and how they operate but there should be a clear, underlying logic in the process.

Inferential statistics Go beyond describing the data for the sample of participants who took part in the study. Inferential statistics are able to determine the probability that the results for the sample are reflective of what might be expected in the broader population from which the sample was drawn. How the sample was chosen and its size are important for deciding whether inferential statistics are appropriate.

Instrumental case study A case study that aims to sharpen a developing theory.

Inter-rater reliability The degree of agreement or consensus among observers.

Interview schedule or interview guide A set of questions developed and used to conduct interviews with people who participate in the research. The questions are designed in such a way that the responses will inform or answer your research questions.

Iterative process Revisiting research questions several times (iterations) to help researchers take broader research questions and gradually narrow the focus to develop specific research questions that delineate more precisely what the research will entail.

Literature review The central purpose of a literature review is to find out what is already known about a specific area of interest and how we know (the design and methods used in previous studies), what still needs to be discovered and how the research builds on previous research or fits into part of a gap left by previous research. The literature review leads into the research question/s guiding the study.

Longitudinal studies There are two types: the first involves collecting data from the same group of participants more than once over an extended period of time; the second involves collecting the same data from successive cohorts over several years.

Measures of central tendency The mean, the mode and the median scores.

Member checking This involves providing opportunities for interviewees to read through the transcripts of their interviews to check for accuracy or for anything that they would like changed or removed before the transcripts are finalised for analysis. Researchers decide in advance whether member checking will be part of their approach. Realistically, it may also depend on how many people will be interviewed and the researcher's timeframe.

Meta-analysis A review of quantitative research in a particular area. The studies reviewed need to conform to certain criteria in order to be included in the review. The aim is to be able to draw conclusions from the combination of a large number of studies in a way that is not possible using single quantitative studies alone.

Mixed-methods research Involves the collection of quantitative and qualitative data, which means that a wide range of skills is needed to plan, implement and report on the research. It can be more difficult to conduct mixed-methods research when the research needs to be small-scale and completed within a short timeframe.

Multiple case study Where the researcher sets out with the intention of examining several cases simultaneously.

Normal distribution Occurs in the shape of a bell curve when the least number of scores falls at the extremes (very high and very low scores) and progressively more scores fall as we move closer to the centre of the distribution, which is where the mean and the median occur for a normal distribution.

Paradigmatic approach This approach to research begins with a paradigm, which influences how the research is approached and the assumptions inherent in how the research questions are asked.

Pragmatic approach Researchers begin with their research questions or their research problems and then select research methods that will address the research questions.

Preliminary (or pilot) project Being small in scale and often limited to relatively few participants, this can be a good starting point for novice researchers. If the opportunity arises, the researcher can build on this valuable experience and extend the participant base in later phases of the study.

Procedural ethics Involves the preparation and submission of formal ethics applications to conduct research. The research must not commence unless and until notification is received that the application for ethical clearance has been approved.

Qualitative research Invites participants to provide responses that involve written and/or spoken words in order to understand a phenomenon or problem from the perspectives of the people involved.

Quantitative research Concerned with data in the form of numbers, such as scores on tests of achievement or when participants rate their responses to a number of questions on a scale.

Quasi-experiment Involves randomly allocating groups such as classes rather than individuals to control and experimental groups. This type of experiment is common in educational settings.

Reflexivity Ongoing reflection on ethical issues and dilemmas, which needs to occur throughout the life of the project, from the planning through to implementation and reporting of the research.

Research design The broad approach or framework employed to investigate or explore a topic or problem. Research designs can be quantitative (for example, experiments) or qualitative, or use mixed methods (combining quantitative and qualitative). Evidence-based research articles may explicitly identify the design used in the study—for example, a case study or particular type of case study or a longitudinal study.

Research participants The people from whom evidence or data are gathered. Participants in quantitative research (in which data are in the form of numbers) are sometimes called subjects.

Research proposal A detailed plan for the research. The exact details required can vary from one university to another, but it will at least include your research questions, the purpose and justification for your study, consideration of the findings of previous research in your area, details of how you will conduct your research, a timeline, schedule of activities and proposed dates.

Sample A sub-section of the population of people who fit into a particular category.

Small-scale research project This should be able to be planned, implemented and reported in writing by a single, busy, novice researcher in a short period of time—perhaps one semester or, for some students, two semesters.

Statistical question Developed from original research questions that indicate a quantitative approach to the research. Statistical questions lead to statistical answers that then enable the original, substantive research question to be answered.

Statistically significant When the results achieved on the dependent variable are at a level that could not have occurred by chance, for example when Method A is concluded to be more effective than Method B.

Surveys A survey can be quantitative or qualitative (Punch, 2003), although a common misperception is that surveys are quantitative only and questionnaires are qualitative. Surveys can involve the collection of quantitative or qualitative data or a combination of both.

Syntax The instructions designed for analysis of data entered into SPSS.

Theory building Involves working inductively and drawing out themes from the data that become the building blocks for theory development. It is commonly associated with qualitative research.

Theory testing Means beginning with a theory that is proposed at the outset and then using quantitative data to test the theory.

Triangulation Involves using more than one method of data collection to answer the research question/s. All methods have their strengths and limitations, so using more than one quantitative or qualitative method or using mixed methods can often help to gain a more complete answer. One method may be more dominant or they could be equally complementary.

Underlying assumptions While some statistical tests may appear to be obvious choices to answer the research question, some—such as correlations—require certain assumptions to be met regarding the data in order for it to be appropriate to use the test. These assumptions are tested with the data first. If the assumptions are met, then the proposed tests can be conducted.

REFERENCES

American Psychological Association (2010), *Publication Manual* (6th ed.), Washington, DC: American Psychological Association.

Bell, J. (2010), *Doing Your Research Project: A guide for first-time researchers in education, health and social sciences* (5th ed.), Maidenhead: Open University Press.

Bennet, M. & Lancaster, J. (2012), Improving Reading in Culturally Situated Contexts, *The Australian Journal of Indigenous Education, 41*(2), pp. 208–17.

Bryman, A. (2016), *Social Research Methods* (5th ed.), Oxford: Oxford University Press.

Campbell, A. & Groundwater-Smith, S. (2007), *An Ethical Approach to Practitioner Research*, New York: Routledge.

Creswell, J.W. (2012), *Educational Research: Planning, conducting and evaluating quantitative or qualitative research* (4th ed.), Boston: Pearson Education.

Davies, M. & Hughes, N. (2014), *Doing a Successful Research Project: Using qualitative or quantitative methods* (2nd ed.), Basingstoke: Palgrave Macmillan.

Guillemin, M. & Gillam, L. (2004), Ethics, Reflexivity, and 'Ethically Important Moments' in Research, *Qualitative Inquiry, 10*(2), pp. 261–80.

Kemmis, S. & McTaggart, R. (eds) (1988), *The Action Research Planner* (3rd ed.), Geelong: Deakin University Press.

Lambert, M. (2012), *A Beginner's Guide to Doing Your Education Research Project*, London: Sage.

Mackenzie, N. & Knipe, S. (2006), Research Dilemmas: Paradigms, methods and methodology, *Issues in Educational Research, 16*(2), pp. 193–205.

McMillan, J.H. & Schumacher, S. (2006), *Research in Education: Evidence-based inquiry* (6th ed.), Boston: Pearson.

—— (2010), *Research in Education: Evidence-based inquiry* (7th ed.), Upper Saddle River, NJ: Pearson Education.

McMillan, J.H. & Wergin, J.F. (2010), *Understanding and Evaluating Educational Research* (4th ed.), Boston: Pearson Education.

Moriarty, B. (2014), Research Design and the Predictive Power of Measures of Self-efficacy, *Issues in Educational Research, 24*(1), pp. 55–66.

Moriarty, B. & Bennet, M. (2016), Practicing Teachers' Reflections: Indigenous Australian student mobility and implications for teacher education, *Social Inclusion, 4*(1), pp. 32–41.

Morrow, V. & Richards, M. (1996), The Ethics of Social Research with Children: An overview, *Children and Society, 10*, pp. 90–105.

Piercy, J. (2014), *The 25 Rules of Grammar: The essential guide to good English*, London: Michael O'Mara Books.

Punch, K.F. & Oancea, A. (2003), *Survey Research: The basics*, London: Sage.

—— (2014), *Introduction to Research Methods in Education* (2nd ed.), London: Sage.

Pyrczak, F. (2017), *Evaluating Research in Academic Journals: A practical guide to realistic evaluation* (6th ed.), Glendale, CA: Pyrczak Publishing.

Wightman, L. & Moriarty, B. (2012), Lifelong Learning and Becoming a Mother: Evaluation of the Young Parents Program, *International Journal of Lifelong Education, 31*(5), pp. 555–67.

INDEX

Made in United States
North Haven, CT
09 July 2024

54582366R00187